HOW SPEAK HOCKEY

Hockey - English
Translation Dictionary

By David John & Brian Kennedy

The Publisher: Arctic Raven

Library and Archives Canada Cataloguing in Publication

John, David, 1977–

   How to speak hockey / David John, Brian Kennedy.

ISBN-13: 978-0-9694977-7-6
ISBN-10: 0-9694977-7-6

   1. Hockey—Dictionaries. 2. Hockey—Terminology.

I. Kennedy, Brian, 1962– II. Title.

GV847.J63 2007   796.96203   C2007-905240-1

Project Director: Yvonne Harris
Project Editor: Nicholle Carrière
Book Design & Layout: Marc Hamm
Cover Design: Joy Dirto
Production: Colin Mcdonald

PC: *P5*

Dedication

To Ewa, who unconditionally supports me
every time I fall.

– David John

Acknowledgments

I would like to thank all those at Arctic Raven for their vision and work on this book. I would also like to thank my friends, who constantly sent me emails and text messages with new words and phrases that I never would have discovered on my own. Thanks to my Ewa for her patience and for listening to me go on and on about how interesting it is to see where these words come from.

I would also like to thank Peter Boer, Brian Kennedy, Terry Jones and Yvonne Harris for their contributions to this book.

Introduction

How does one speak hockey? For hockey fans who grew up playing street hockey and watching their favorite team, understanding a phrase such as "He blasted a howitzer from the hash marks" comes naturally, but those who do not speak the language of hockey would have no idea that it meant "to shoot the puck really hard from the lines of the faceoff circle."

The language of hockey is ever changing and evolving. From the first time an organized game was played in the distant past to the bright lights of today's modern NHL teams, if hockey players from the two eras were to talk about the game, each would have great difficulty understanding what the other person meant. Take the basic description of an opening faceoff for example.

Opening faceoff 1881: "Two hockeyists lineup with their hurleys at the ready. The umpire skates in for the opening bully. He faces the puck, and the match is under way."

Opening faceoff 2001: "Welcome hockey fans. The opening faceoff is brought to you by McDonalds restaurants. The 22,000 fans are in full swing as the players lineup for the opening faceoff. The camera zooms in on center ice, the referee drops the puck and the game is underway."

As far as the game has come, the language of hockey had to start somewhere, and the words we use today have some strange and fascinating origins.

The Origins of Hockey

To learn how to speak the language of hockey, it helps to look back to the origins of the sport and how it developed into the fast-paced game of the present day. There are many cities in Canada, and even some countries on the other side of the pond, that have laid claim to being the birthplace of hockey, but unfortunately for these cities' tourist industries, the origins of our beloved sport are a tad more complicated.

And Hockey God said, "Let there be ice", and there was ice. And Hockey God said, "Let there be five players per team, sticks, skates, goaltenders and a referee," and so it was.

No, hockey was not born of the gods. It took years for the game to develop from its roots into its modern form.

The origins of the game can be traced to a similar-sounding Irish game called hurling. Hurling is a fast-paced sport played on a field of grass with ax-shaped sticks and a ball. The problem with hurling is that it came from a country that had grass to play on year round, but in Canada, the harsh winters forced the players to hang up their sticks until spring. Writer Garth Vaughan attributes the move of hurling from grass fields to ice to students attending King's College School in Windsor, Nova Scotia. Whenever they had free time, the students would make their way down to the local skating spot, clear away the snow and play their new game. But it still wasn't called hockey. Eventually the game began to catch on, and as it spread and became more organized, a set of rules began to evolve, giving the game its own unique character.

The first official rules of hockey:

- The game was played with a block of wood for a puck. The puck was not allowed to leave the ice.

- The stones marking the goals were placed on the ice at opposite angles to where the goals are in present-day hockey.

- There was to be no slashing.

- Players were not allowed to lift their sticks above the shoulder.

- When a goal was scored, the teams changed ends.

- Players had to keep on side.

- Forward passing was permitted.

- Players played the whole game.

- There was a no-replacement rule.

- The game had two 30-minute periods, with one 10-minute break in between.

- The goalkeeper had to stand for the entire game.

As the game became more popular and more organized, the language of the game began to evolve as well. Wooden pucks and "road apples" were replaced with vulcanized rubber pucks; hockey moved from frozen, windswept ponds to fully climate-controlled ice palaces; carved, wooden, one-piece hockey sticks with straight blades evolved into laminated, curved and eventually composite sticks; and the game has gone from a sport played on local rinks in North America to a global institution played by millions.

Few realize the impact of hockey-speak on our shared culture. Politicians talk of elections as if they were announcing a Saturday night game between the Montreal Canadiens and the Toronto Maple Leafs. They refer to elections going into overtime and sending misbehaving politicians to the penalty box. The iconic Zamboni machine is found in everything from *Peanuts* comic strips (for those of you who don't know, the little yellow bird Woodstock cleared his frozen bird feeder with a Zamboni) to the popular 1980s television series *Cheers* (the Zamboni was responsible for the death of Carla's hockey-playing second husband, Eddie).

Anyone can speak the language of hockey. In fact, most of us already know a few words and, even if we don't realize it, use them as part of how we interact on a daily basis. I have compiled a comprehensive list of the language that surrounds the game; some words will be familiar to you, and some will completely surprise you.

And for the completely uninitiated, if any of what you have just read still does not register, then please keep reading and immerse yourself in the often strange, confusing and wonderful world of hockey-speak.

A: The letter found on the jersey of the player designated the team's assistant captain.

Altercation: A polite word for a fight or a pushing match. "The two players involved in the altercation were sent to the sin bin for five minutes to cool down."

Arena: The name for the building in which hockey is played. When hockey first began, games were played on outdoor rinks subject to the whims of the weather, but gradually hockey began to move indoors, and the hockey arena was born. However, as many hockey moms and dads can attest to, it is sometimes colder in the arena than it is outside.

Armor: The foam-and-plastic protection worn by players under their jerseys. When players first started wearing padding to protect themselves, it was nothing more than dense foam and leather, but as the game got faster and players

A

got bigger, the padding became more rigid and armor-like. The chest protectors that goaltenders wear even look somewhat like bulletproof armor.

Around the world glove save: When a goaltender swings his arm in a circular motion and snags the puck out of midair. Netminder Patrick Roy was always the best at exaggerating this little piece of goaltender magic.

Assist: In most cases, when a goal is scored, a point is awarded to the one or two players who last touched the puck before the goal was scored as well as to the scorer. A maximum of two assists is allowed per goal.

Attacking zone: Also "offensive zone." The area of the ice in which one team is on the defense and the other is on the offense looking to score.

B

Back checking: When one team loses the puck in the opponent's zone, and the forwards must hurry back to their end to stop the other team from scoring.

Back door: With a team in the offensive zone, the back door is the area near the net behind the defensemen. A player is said to be "sneaking in the back door" when he gets in behind the defense and is left alone in front of the goaltender.

Backstop: The goaltender.

Backyard rink: Across the frozen North, children learn to skate on the ice of the backyard rink. Many of today's National Hockey League players took their first steps towards the professional ranks on the rinks behind their houses, the most famous of them being the Great One himself, Wayne Gretzky. The story of how young Wayne Gretzky got from his backyard rink in Brantford, Ontario, to the top of professional hockey is part

B

of hockey lore and a large part of how Canadians identify with the game.

Built in large part so that Wayne's dad, Walter Gretzky, would not have to freeze to death down at the local rink, "Wally's Coliseum," as it was known as, served the young protégé well. According to Wayne, "I used to go out after school for an hour and a half, and then I'd come in to eat dinner, and when it came time to go out again, I'd be sitting there and he'd say, 'You didn't do any shooting or practicing.' And I'd say, 'I didn't feel like it.' And he'd say, 'Well, someday, you may have to get up at six-thirty and go to work from seven to five, and you'd better feel like it.' Little things like that would give me the motivation."

Hockey parents across the country build these rinks in the hopes that their kids will one day grow up to be just like Wayne Gretzky, keeping the tradition of the backyard rink alive for generations to come.

Badgering: Referees everywhere are very familiar with badgering. When a player disagrees with a call a referee has made, the player will often argue with the ref until play is resumed. This incessant arguing is called badgering.

Banana blade: When the curved stick was first introduced into the National Hockey League in the 1960s, the curve in the blade was so pronounced that it resembled a banana.

Barn: A hockey arena.

Bench-clearing brawl: The rarest type of brawl in hockey. This is when everybody on the ice and on the benches gets involved in one large fighting extravaganza. To avoid such brawls, the National Hockey League imposes heavy fines and penalties for any player leaving the bench to join a fight on the ice.

One of the most famous bench-clearing brawls occurred between the Quebec Nordiques and the Montreal Canadiens on April 20, 1984, and is referred to as the "Good Friday Brawl." The hatred between the two teams had been building for years and finally exploded during the playoffs after a Nordiques player instigated the brawl with a vicious hit to a Montreal player. Both teams' benches cleared instantly, and referees had a difficult time restoring order and picking up all the equipment littering the ice.

Bench minor: A penalty given to either a coach, player or trainer for the use of offensive language

B

toward the officials, for throwing objects onto the ice or for interfering with the progress of the game. A player is selected by the coaching staff to serve a two-minute penalty for the infraction.

Between the pipes: When hockey was first played on the ponds of rural Canada, the only objects that could be found to mark the goal area were usually large rocks. Eventually, as the game became more organized, rocks were no longer considered appropriate to demarcate the goal and were replaced by metal pipes. So today, a goaltender standing in his crease is said to be standing between the pipes.

Biscuit: The puck.

Biscuit in the basket: While biscuit is another term for puck, basket is another term for the hockey net. Putting a biscuit in the basket simply means to score a goal.

Blades: Normally refers to the sharp steel under the boot of the skate, but this term is also commonly used to describe the whole skate.

Blast: A very hard slapshot aimed at the goalie.

Blind pass: When a player passes the puck to a teammate without looking. This does not always work in the professional ranks, but when it does, the play will certainly make the highlight reels.

B

Blocker: The glove worn on a goaltender's stick hand. It has a rectangular board, often curved up at one end, attached to the backhand side. One of the later additions to the world of hockey, the blocker is now an essential piece of equipment in the goaltenders' war on the puck. However, when it was first introduced, some NHL coaches vehemently protested its use.

In the early days of hockey, goaltenders had to make do with gloves that were almost identical to those of the forwards and defensemen. Looking at the old black-and-white photos of early NHL goaltenders such as Clint Benedict, Georges Hainsworth and Lorne Chabot, they all had slightly modified players' gloves with added padding over the hands for protection. Remarkably, it wasn't until the 1947–48 NHL regular season that one innovative goaltender decided to try something new.

Like a kid improvising equipment for a street hockey game, Chicago Blackhawks goaltender Emile "the Cat" Francis wanted to increase the protection on his stick hand, so he taped an outer layer of dense sponge rubber to his glove.

How to Speak Hockey

B

This gave Francis the extra protection he was looking for, and it reduced the amount of open net for the shooter. The league quickly approved it, and soon all the goaltenders had added this weapon to their arsenal.

Blue liner: A defenseman. Defensemen are dubbed "blue liners" because they spend most of their time on the ice standing on the blue line.

Boarding: When a player violently pushes an opponent into the boards. Boarding normally occurs when a player is pushed headfirst from behind into the boards. A player who receives two boarding penalties during the course of the regular season or the playoffs receives an automatic one game suspension. Boarding can be a minor or major penalty at the referee's discretion, based on the degree of violence of the action.

Boots: Skates.

Brain bucket: A helmet.

Branch: An old hockey term for a stick. It's a very fitting reference, because the first hockey sticks were carved out of a single piece of wood usually taken from the branch of a hardwood tree.

Brawl: Hockey players fight, but they don't often brawl. In a brawl everybody on the ice is involved in fighting. Brawls have been a part of hockey since the game began, and hockey is not likely to ever be without them. Even the goal-tenders get in on the action when there is a brawl. Because goaltenders are less mobile, they usually fight each other to even the odds.

Breakaway: When a player gets the puck and has an open run at the goaltender—something that's always guaranteed to get fans on their feet. Along with the penalty shot, a breakaway is one of the most exciting moments in hockey.

Maurice Richard was one of the best breakaway players in the game. When asked what the fondest memory of his hockey career was, Toronto Maple Leafs goaltender Johnny Bower said, "The day the Rocket retired!"

Break out: When a team gains control of the puck in their defensive end, they will "break out" of their zone with the puck to go on the attack. Most teams have established break-out plays to accomplish this important part of the game.

Break the ice: When a team scores the first goal in a game, they have broken the ice.

B

B

Break-shins: This term alludes to the violent nature of the early form of the game. There were many early accounts of "hurley-on-ice" leading to broken teeth, cut lips and bruised shins. In an era before proper padding, calling the game "break-shins" seemed natural because many boys returned home from the pond with bruises all over their legs.

Brouhaha: A major confrontation among players that almost clears the bench.

Brick wall: What every goaltender aspires to be. The "brick wall" is the elusive quality that some goaltenders have, seemingly able to stop every shot as if a brick wall had been constructed on the goal line of the net.

Terry Sawchuk was the best bricklayer in NHL history, putting up a wall in front of his net for 103 career shutouts. Goaltender Nikolai Khabibulin was so successful at stopping pucks early in his career that he earned himself the nickname the "Bulin Wall."

Bury the puck: When the puck is shot hard into the back of the net, it has been "buried." Often used when there is traffic in front of the goal, and the puck still manages to find its way into the net.

Butterfly goaltending: The term "butterfly" refers to a style of goaltending in which the goaltender drops to his knees on the ice and extends his legs parallel to the goal line to take away the bottom of the net from the shooter; the goaltender's legs are extended like the wings of a butterfly. As to why it was called butterfly and not something more masculine is a mystery. Since 70 percent of all shots on goal are aimed at the lower half of the net, butterfly goaltending has become the prevailing style used by National Hockey League goaltenders.

The style was developed in the 1960s by goal-tending legend Glenn Hall. During the era when goaltenders did not wear masks, it was danger-ous for the goalie to crouch low in the net and expose his face to the puck. At first, Hall was lauded for his courage for dropping to his knees to make saves, exposing himself to injury, but Hall insisted that he developed the style to avoid injuries. By using the butterfly position, Hall did not have to dive after stray pucks and put his face in a vulnerable position. The butterfly allowed him to cover the length of the net without relying on an acrobatic and potentially dangerous save. Hall was not without his share of facial injuries, but the butterfly style probably

B

B

saved him from some of the over 400 stitches that his contemporary, Terry Sawchuk, received to his face over the course of his career.

But the goaltender that truly popularized the butterfly style, and the main reason it is practiced so widely in the NHL today, was Patrick Roy. Almost every save Roy made was in the butterfly position, and because he used it so effectively, it was copied by most of his colleagues in the NHL and all the way down to peewee goaltending schools. Few have been able to equal Roy's effectiveness with the style, but it still remains predominant in goaltending circles.

Butt-ending: Similar to spearing. Using the end of the shaft of the stick in a jabbing motion on another player. As with spearing, the player earns an automatic major and game misconduct penalty.

Buzzer: The siren that sounds at the end of each period.

Buzzer beater: A goal that is scored with only a few seconds remaining in the period; also, when a team that is trailing by a goal near the end of a game scores the tying goal.

C

C: The letter found on the jersey of the player designated the team captain. The captaincy is usually given to the senior member of the team who best displays leadership qualities to other players.

Cage: The goal net.

Cannon: A very hard slapshot.

Carom: When the puck rebounds or ricochets off the boards or any other object on the ice, players included.

Catch iron: When the puck hits the goalposts.

Center: The forward whose job it is to play the center position on the ice. The center takes faceoffs and is the leader on the attack.

Center ice: The area at the center of the rink where the puck is dropped at the beginning of each period or after every goal.

C

Change up: A shot that fools the goaltender. The term is borrowed from baseball. The goaltender thinks the puck will come in fast, but the shooter either doesn't get enough power behind the shot or else the puck deflects off another player along the way, slowing it down.

Changing on the fly: The changing of players on the ice while the play continues. Changing on the fly never occurs when the opposing team is in control of the puck or when the puck is in the defensive zone, which would give the other team the advantage. When changing on the fly, the players must be careful to avoid putting too many men on the ice. Sometimes in the confusion of changing lines, one extra player will remain on the ice, and if the referee notices the infraction, he will assess a two-minute minor penalty.

Charging: An infraction that occurs when a player takes three or more strides or leaves his feet before checking an opponent. A two-minute penalty is assessed.

Cheap-shot artist: The most hated of players in hockey circles. Cheap-shot artists hit, punch, jab, trip and injure other players, usually when the other guy is not looking, and they are often the

How to Speak Hockey

first to plead their innocence to the referees. One of the most notorious cheap-shot artists was Bryan Marchment. Countless times during his career, Marchment would intentionally go knee on knee with the stars of the league and was responsible for many players being unable to play because of injury.

Cherry picking: When a player remains near the opponent's attacking zone and waits for an outlet pass, hoping to get a breakaway on net.

Chest protector: Since the puck was rarely shot above waist level in the early days of hockey, it was unnecessary for a goaltender to have any protection on his chest. But as players got better, shots became harder, and increasingly, goaltenders would crouch lower to make a save, they needed something to protect their chests. The first chest protectors were actually borrowed from baseball catchers and protected the chest and shoulders, with an extra flap to cover the groin area. The modern chest protector looks more like a bulletproof vest than a puck stopper, but because some players can shoot the puck over 100 miles per hour, goaltenders need every piece of padding they can get.

Chicklets: Teeth.

C

Chip shot: When a player passes the puck without any real control over the direction and very little power. Chipping the puck is considered a very conservative style, as this type of shot makes it difficult to begin a formal rush towards the opposing team, and it is likely that they will get possession.

Chippy: When a player is irritated and ready for a fight.

Chirping: The sound a referee hears when a player argues a penalty call. Many expletives are typically used in chirping.

Circle the wagons: When a player skates into the offensive zone, goes around the net, avoiding all other players, and comes up the other side. It is not the most strategic move, but it can be effective if the opposing team takes the bait and pursues the player. However, what most often occurs is that the player loses the puck, resulting in a turnover.

Clear the puck: When a player in his own defensive zone shoots the puck the length of the ice to relieve pressure from the opposing team's attack.

Clothesline: When one player sticks out his arms and strikes another, unsuspecting player in the head, knocking him to the ground.

C

Clubhouse lawyer: A player in the dressing room who always seems to be involved in everybody's business and has an opinion on everything.

Clutch and grab: A game in which either one or both teams are constantly hooking or holding the opposition in order to slow them down. This style of hockey is rarely seen today because of stricter enforcement of the rules.

Coast to coast: Also "end to end." When a player starts with the puck in his own defensive end and skates all the way to the other end of the ice, never once passing the puck.

Composite sticks: For over 100 years, hockey players relied on wooden sticks, which served them well, but by the 1980s, companies were beginning to experiment with materials other than wood. In the late 1980s, Wayne Gretzky was the first to relinquish his reliable wooden stick for an aluminum one. The lighter stick allowed players to shoot quicker, and the stiffer nature of aluminum provided a better transfer of energy

C

to the puck for harder shots. Another revolution in stick technology occurred at the end of the 20th century with the development of composite graphite and Kevlar sticks. Though the sticks weighed just 16.2 ounces, players found that the combination of the strength of the shaft and its ability to flex increased the speed of their shots considerably, much to the chagrin of goaltenders around the league. Today, the majority of NHL players have made the switch to composite sticks, but there are still a few holdouts that have kept their wooden ones.

Cord cottage: The goal net.

Corral the puck: A colorful way of describing how a player accepts a hard pass. When a player shoots a hard pass to a teammate, the receiver must corral the puck on his stick.

Couple of quicks: Two fast goals scored at the start of a game or the beginning of a period.

Cover point: A term used in the early days of hockey when seven men played on the ice. The defensemen played in two positions, cover point and point. Cover point was played in front of the point, acting as the first line of defense.

Crease: The blue area in front of the goal.

Cross-checking: When a player lifts his stick off the ice, holds it in front of his body parallel to his shoulders and smashes it into an opposing player. A referee will not always call a cross-checking penalty when a player (normally a defenseman) lightly cross-checks a player in front of the goal crease. For obvious cross-checking offenses, a minor or major penalty can be assessed on the player, depending on the end result of the check.

Crossover: A skating technique in which one foot is placed in front of ("crossed over") the other. Crossovers can be done while skating forward or backward, and it is one of the essential skating techniques taught to children at a young age, helping them to negotiate corners at a higher speed.

Cue: A hockey stick. The term is borrowed from the game of pool.

Cupping: When a player illegally closes his hand around the puck.

Curved sticks: The curved stick was invented in the 1960s, when Chicago Blackhawk Stan Mikita cracked the blade of his stick during a practice.

C

Since it was just a practice and the tape still held the blade together, he kept playing with the stick and found that the puck did some strange things with the new curve to the blade. The curve made the puck go in all different directions, curving through the air and making it very difficult for the goaltenders to follow. Teammate Bobby Hull tried out the blade and decided he wanted one of his own, finding that his shot was much more unpredictable and a lot harder than normal. Overnight, Mikita and Hull bent their stick blades in water, and the banana blade was born. But after several years, the league stepped in and decided that the extra curve gave forwards an unfair advantage, so they made a new rule allowing a curve of no more than half an inch. During their days of playing with the curved sticks, Mikita and Hull remained at the top of the scoring leaders in the NHL.

Custodian of the cord cottage: The goaltender.

Cycle the puck: When in the attacking zone, the offensive team will alternate possession of the puck in the corners, keeping the opposition on their toes. The player with the puck will swoop into the corner while his teammate circles around to the other side and returns to the corner to take the puck from his teammate.

D

Dance: When two players lovingly embrace, hold each other by the shoulders, move around the ice gracefully and rain bare-knuckle punches down on one another.

Dasher: The lower part of the boards that surround the rink. Different rinks have different color dashers.

Defenseman: The defenseman is one of two players on a team whose responsibility it is to defend their zone and net from opposing players.

Defensive zone: The area behind the blue line becomes the defensive zone when a team must defend their goal from the attacking team.

Deke: Also "fake-out." When the puck carrier fools another player or goaltender to get the puck past him.

Delayed offside: If a player enters the offensive zone ahead of the puck but does not touch it,

D

the play is offside, but no whistle is blown immediately. The linesman will raise his arms to signal the offside, and if the player does not leave the zone, the linesman will whistle the offside.

Delay of game: Any action that the referee believes slows the progress of the game, resulting in a delay of game minor penalty. The following cases are considered a delay of game:

- A player or goaltender deliberately shoots or throws the puck outside the playing area

- A player or goaltender intentionally pushes the net out of its normal position

- A team delays putting the right number of players on the ice for a faceoff

- A player or goaltender stops play to adjust equipment

- A player deliberately falls or gathers the puck underneath him

- A player closes his hand on the puck

- The puck is not kept in motion by a player or goaltender

Denied (a goal): A player is denied a goal when a goalie makes a difficult save on the shooter. Usually the shooter will have an open net, but the goaltender somehow manages to stop the puck. Denied!

Dent the mesh: To score a goal.

Dig: When the puck gets caught in the corner of the rink and several players try to gain possession, they have to "dig" the puck out of the mess of players, skates and sticks.

Dipsy doodle: The same as a fake-out or a deke, but the move is a lot fancier.

Disc: The puck.

Dish: A well-executed pass.

Dive: When a player intentionally falls to the ice to draw a penalty against an opposing player, he is said to be taking a dive. In the early days of hockey, diving was known as "fainting."

Doing the needful: A term used in the 1800s to describe scoring a goal.

Donut: A shutout; a score of zero points.

D

Doorstep: The area directly in front of the goaltender. Announcers often will say that a player is "right on the doorstep."

Down low: In the attacking zone, down low is the area behind the net and the goal line. It is essential for a team to be able to win the battles "down low" in the corners of the rink to come up with the puck and possibly get a chance to score.

Draw: A faceoff.

Drop pass: When a player going forward passes the puck backwards without looking at the intended recipient.

Dump-in: When an attacking team shoots the puck into the corner of the opponent's zone instead of carrying the puck in and taking the chance of being stripped of the puck.

Dump and chase: A style of hockey in which a team constantly throws the puck into the opposing team's end and attempts to gain control of the puck by sending more players into the corners. Not the most popular style of hockey, but it can prove effective against some teams.

E

Elbowing: When a player uses his elbow to hit another player. Usually a major penalty is awarded because use of the elbow is seen as intentional.

Eleven months of winter and one month of bad skating: A phrase used to describe to the country of Canada.

Empty-net goal: When a goaltender is pulled in favor of putting in an extra attacker, and the opposing team is able to put the puck into the empty net for a goal.

"With just 45 seconds remaining in the game, the Boston Bruins have removed their goaltender and sent in an extra attacker. The Bruins need one goal to tie the Canadiens and send the game into overtime. The Bruins dump the puck into the Canadiens' zone. Several players chase the puck into the corner. The Bruins are desperately trying to dig the puck out from the Canadiens defense-man's skates, but it is the Canadiens who come up with the puck. The Canadiens move the puck out into the neutral zone, and their star player aims for the open net and...scores! The Canadiens put the game away on an empty-net goal and win the game 5–3."

End to end: Also "coast to coast." When a player starts with the puck in his own defensive end and skates all the way to the other end of the ice, never once passing the puck.

Enforcer: The player on a team whose job it is to protect the team's stars. The enforcer is an essential member of any team with a superstar player and is expected to rough up or fight any opponent who dares intimidate his teammates.

Extra attacker: When the referee calls a penalty and the offending team does not have possession of the puck, the official raises his hand to signal the infraction but cannot whistle the play dead until a player from the offending team touches the puck. When this occurs, the goaltender from the non-penalized team is allowed to leave the ice and be replaced by another player, the extra attacker, until the whistle is blown. This gives the team a sort of mini power play until the offending team can stop the play by touching the puck.

E

F

F

Faceoff: Also called the "draw." The faceoff may appear to have a simple definition but putting it into practice can be a complicated procedure. Simply, the faceoff is used to start the play at the beginning of each period, after a goal is scored and after any stoppage in play. One player from each team approaches the faceoff area, gets into position and waits for the ref or linesman to drop the puck. The winner of the faceoff is the team that gets possession of the puck. In the early days of hockey, the referee would "face" the puck at center ice, while the players lined up for the opening "bully." As odd as it sounds, this was how the faceoff was described when hockey was still in its infancy.

Originally, the puck was placed on the ice between two players, and once the referee yelled "play," only then could the battle for the puck or faceoff take place. It was referee legend Fred Waghorne who first dropped the puck on the faceoff to avoid the fighting between the players as they waited for the referee to yell "play" to start the faceoff. Waghorne was the first to position the players about a foot apart and have them keep their sticks on the ice until the puck was dropped. From then on, the rules were changed so that players were prohibited from body contact prior to the dropping of the puck. Other players not taking the faceoff had to stay at least 15 feet from the puck, and all players had to be onside.

There are nine official faceoff spots on the ice, one at center ice, two on each side of the neutral zone and two inside each defensive zone. However, not all faceoffs are taken on the designated faceoff circles. Faceoffs can occur anywhere on the ice where an infraction has taken place. For example, if a player shoots the puck over the boards from the neutral zone, the ensuing faceoff takes place from the spot where the player shot the puck into the crowd. A player can also be thrown out of a faceoff for trying to gain an advantage on the other player by shifting his position.

It is essential for teams to have a reliable player with a good faceoff-win percentage. For example, when a team is winning by one goal with very little time remaining in the game, it is essential to win every possible faceoff and keep the puck off the sticks of the opposing team to prevent them from scoring. Winning a faceoff is not easy, and those that are good at it have made it into an art form.

Face wash: If a player wants to try to draw a penalty on an opponent or just get him really angry, he will rub his sweat- and spit-covered glove in the opponent's face as if he is trying to get a mustard stain off. Not the most pleasant experience. Face washing usually occurs when players are involved in a pushing and shoving match, often just after a whistle in front of the net.

Fagging: A strange word to find in the hockey lexicon, but it actually means to back check. Fagging was a term used in the first few decades of hockey to describe a forward skating back into his own zone to stop the other team from getting a chance on goal.

Fake-out: Also "deke." A maneuver in which the puck carrier fools another player or goaltender to get the puck past him.

Fan: When a player winds up to take a shot and misses the puck completely. One of the lighter moments in hockey. The term "fan" is used because the player creates a nice breeze with his stick instead of transferring the energy to the puck.

Far side: The opposite side of the ice to a shooter as he comes into the attacking zone along the boards to the right or the left of the goaltender.

F

Farm team: An essential part of a professional hockey league. A farm team is always affiliated with an NHL team and is the training ground for its young talent. When a player is sent back to the farm, he is being sent down to the minor leagues to train up to the standards of the NHL. Having a good farm team is essential to the survival of the big brother NHL franchise if it wants a constant supply of talent when older players retire or the team suffers a wave of injuries.

Fifty-fifty (50-50): A type of raffle popular at hockey games. Spectators purchase tickets during the early part of the game, and the winner is announced during the second intermission.

The real reason the 57,167 fans at the Edmonton Heritage Classic outdoor game in Common-wealth Stadium in 2003 hung in there until the third period of the game between the Oilers and Montreal Canadiens in −16°F temperatures was that the lucky number for the 50-50 hadn't been announced yet. Payout totals for the 50-50, with half the money going to minor hockey and other charities, for regular season games in Edmonton are usually near $30,000.

Firewagon hockey: No, this is not a bunch of burning wagons on the ice. This term is used to describe an all-out offensive approach to the game. In firewagon hockey, teams are less concerned with defending their own nets and instead focus on putting pucks into the opposing team's net. This brand of hockey was popular in the 1980s.

With the arrival of Wayne Gretzky and his highly skilled Edmonton Oilers teammates, goal production significantly increased in the National Hockey League from the 1970s through the 1980s. During the 1977–78 regular season, Ken Dryden led all goaltenders with the lowest goals-against average at 2.05. Fast forward to the 1986–87 season, and the goaltender with the lowest goals-against average was Montreal Canadien Brian Hayward, with an average of 2.81, followed by teammate Patrick Roy, with a 2.93 average. With a team such as Edmonton

scoring a record 446 goals, an average of
5.6 goals per game in the 1983–84 season,
"firewagon hockey" was the best way to describe
the style of play that had games ending with
scores of 8–1, 10–5 and 12–7.

While the 1980s exemplified firewagon hockey,
the term came into being in the late 1940s and
was popular through to the Montreal Canadiens
five straight Stanley Cups of the late 1950s.
Beginning with the arrival of players such as
Maurice Richard and Gordie Howe in the 1940s,
offense on the ice opened up scoring and
ushered in the glory days of the National Hockey
League. While many teams still held on to strict
defensive principles, the Montreal Canadiens
were proponents of a type of hockey that
earned their players the nickname "Flying
Frenchmen" because of their attacking style.
With a number one lineup that consisted of
Maurice Richard, Elmer Lach and Toe Blake,
dubbed the "Punch Line," it was just a matter of
time before the rest of the league adopted the
Canadiens' style just to be able to keep up on
the scoreboard. Although the Canadiens did not
win the Cup in the 1944–45 season, Maurice
Richard scored an incredible 50 goals in 50 games,
finishing with his linemates in the top three in

F

overall scoring. The Toronto Maple Leafs defensive style of hockey dominated to the end of the 1940s, but players such as Gordie Howe, Dickie Moore, Jean Beliveau, Ted Lindsay and Henri Richard could not be kept at bay forever, and fans got to watch some of the most exciting hockey in the game's history.

Fish out of water: When a goaltender is caught completely out of position and throws his body in any direction to make a save, looking somewhat like a fish flopping around on the ice. This maneuver does not get much respect from fans or broadcasters, but it can sometimes be effective as a desperation move (just ask Dominic Hasek, who is well known for his fish out of water–type saves).

Fisticuffs: A fight.

Five-hole: The area between the goaltender's legs. One of the seven positions or "holes" that a goalie must protect. See "holes."

Flash the leather: A glove save by a goaltender. The term is still used, though goaltenders' gloves or trappers are no longer made out of leather. A goaltender flashes the leather when a shooter blasts a shot to an open part of the net, and the goaltender quickly whips his glove around to make the save. Patrick Roy was well known for overemphasizing his glove saves. When the puck was simply shot into his glove, he would still "flash the leather" as if he had made a fantastic save.

Flip pass: A pass in which the puck is lifted over an obstacle to reach the intended recipient. For example, if two players break in on goal on a two-on-one play, and one player wants to pass the puck to the other but the defenseman is blocking his passing lane, then he can a attempt a flip pass. It is used frequently in fast-break situations.

Floater: A very weak shot that arches in towards the goal.

Forechecking: When one team is in possession of the puck and is trying to get out of their defensive zone to start a rush up the ice, and the opposing team sends in one or two players to stop them in what is referred to as the "fore-check." Usually one player pesters the puck carrier, trying to pressure him into making a mistake and hopefully turning over the puck to give the opposing team a scoring chance.

F

Forward: The general name for players in attacking positions. The two forwards are the main goal scorers on the team. Forward positions are left winger, right winger and center.

Four-on-four: When two penalties are called against one player on each team, both teams continue playing for the duration of the penalty with just four players. For two minutes, both teams play four-on-four hockey.

Freeze: The ice.

Freeze the puck: When players hold the puck against the boards with either their sticks or their skates in order to get the referee to whistle the play dead. Goaltenders can also freeze the puck when a loose disc enters the goal crease. Freezing the puck outside the goal crease can earn a player a two-minute minor penalty.

G

Gallery gods: Fans in the nosebleeds or upper decks. The term originated to describe fans in the old Boston Garden, but it is now used throughout the hockey world. Gallery gods are also known as "real fans" in the modern-day game because lower bowl seats are almost entirely bought up by corporations.

Game ho!: No one alive would remember celebrating a goal by screaming "Game ho!" but that's exactly what hockey players shouted in the first few decades of the game when they put a puck in the net.

Game on!: Heard frequently during street hockey games, players will yell "Game on!" after a car has passed and the game can resume.

Game misconduct: A penalty that is usually imposed when a player intentionally attempts to injure another player. The offending player is suspended for the remainder of a game, and a substitute player is allowed to replace the penalized player. A game misconduct carries an automatic fine of $200, and the case is reported to the NHL Commissioner, who can impose further fines or a suspension from upcoming games.

G

Garbage goal: A goal that does not take much effort or talent to score. This type of goal is often scored when a goaltender lets out a juicy rebound (see "rebound") or is out of position.

Gates: The doors that open onto the ice from a team's bench. "The players came out of the gates fighting."

Gauntlets: Hockey gloves. For many years, hockey players did not wear gloves of any kind, and if they did, they often wore just a regular pair of leather winter gloves. But as the game developed and the play became faster and more violent, players needed something to protect their hands from errant sticks. Some of the first gloves used in hockey were actually cricket gloves. The gloves protected the hands from slashing but were not made to accommodate the range of movement needed by hockey players. The first version of gauntlets specifically tailored for hockey did not appear until 1904, when Eaton's department store began selling them in their catalog for $1.75.

The basic construction of the hockey glove has changed little over the years. The biggest difference has been in the materials used to protect the players' hands from injuries. In the past, gloves were made mostly of foam padding and leather, but modern hockey players wear gloves made from hard plastic and dense foam covered in nylon, which offer better protection against slashes and the occasional skate blade.

Give and go: A passing exchange between two players on the attack. The players pass the puck to each other quickly so as not to give the defenders or the goaltender any indication which player is going to shoot the puck.

Goal crease: The painted area directly in front of the net. NHL regulations state that the goal crease must measure 8 feet wide and 6 feet deep. Players are generally allowed to enter the goal crease, but if they come into contact with the goaltender, they can be charged with a two-minute goaltender interference penalty.

Goal judge: With the abundance of cameras that are now focused on the ice, it seems rather pointless to continue the tradition of the goal judge, but at one time, goal judges were the most important officials on the ice. Called "goal umpires" in the early days of hockey, they were an essential part of the game when hockey goals had no nets and there were no cameras for instant replay. The goal used to be defined by just two simple poles stuck in the ice, which made it rather difficult at times to decipher if the puck had actually crossed the line on the front side of the goal. Add to that the fact that players would often crash the through the goal, sending bodies flying over the goal line at the same time as the puck, making the goal judge's decisions the source of much scrutiny and controversy. When nets were finally introduced into the game, the goal judge moved from his spot directly behind the net to a little perch behind the boards. In the days before instant replay, given the importance of the goal judge's decisions, the judge was often the target of aggression from both players and fans.

One famous incident involved a goal judge, Montreal Canadiens legend Aurel Joliat and a mob of angry fans. Joliat crashed in front of the goal and, to the best of his knowledge, put the puck past the goaltender and into the net, but the goal judge did not see it that way and refused to call the goal. Joliat immediately flew into a rage, jumped over the boards and began to rain down blows on the poor judge. But the official's ordeal was far from over, because after Joliat was pulled off the judge, fans broke open the gate of his booth and tried to finish the job that the Canadiens player had started. The battered and bruised judge had to be removed from the arena under police escort.

Today the goal judge's job is a lot less controversial and definitely a lot less dangerous. A modern-day goal judge simply signals whether the puck has passed completely over the goal line with the push of a button that turns on a red light. It is not the goal judge's job to decide whether or not a goal was legally scored. This is left to the discretion of the referee or the video goal judge who can overturn the goal judge's decision at any time.

Goaltender interference: When an attacking player either impedes a goaltender's ability to make a save or comes into more than incidental contact with the netminder. For as long as there have been goaltenders in the net, players have been getting in their way. Throughout the history of the league, goalies have long complained that the NHL does not use the goaltender interference penalty for their protection. During the 1998–99 NHL season, the league attempted to protect goaltenders by disallowing any player from entering into the goaltender's crease at the front of the net. If so much as a toe was in the goal crease when a goal was scored, it was automatically disallowed regardless of whether or not the goaltender was interfered with. Luckily, that rule was abolished before the start of the next season.

Goal mouth: The area just in front of the goal line and behind the goal line inside the net.

Goal suck: A term heard more often during street hockey games and in local arenas rather than in the professional ice palaces of the NHL, a goal suck is a player that always stays within striking distance of the opponent's net. Though this type of player is generally not very well respected, he always seems to manage a break on goal from time to time.

Goalie/Goaltender: The player whose job it is to stand in front of the net and stop the opposing team from scoring. A goalie is typically covered from head to toe in padding for protection against the puck.

Gobble up the puck: When either team has a chance at the puck and someone takes possession of it.

Golden opportunity: An excellent scoring chance.

Goon: A player who cannot skate very well, does not have much of a shot, is much bigger than the average player and whose sole purpose is to start and finish fights. Very few goons remain in hockey these days, but those who grew up watching hockey in the 1970s would be well aware of the term. Among the more notable goons in hockey history were Sprague Cleghorn, Dave "Tiger" Williams, Dave Schultz and Tie Domi. A goon should not be confused with an enforcer. A goon will set out to injure, while the job of the enforcer is to protect his teammates.

Goose egg: A colorful term for a shutout, that is, a score of zero points.

Gordie Howe hat trick: Gordie Howe was well known for his ability to put the puck into the net, but he could fight as easily as he could score. To make a Gordie Howe hat trick, a player must score a goal, get an assist and get into a fight all in the same game.

G

Grinder: A player who works best in the corners, digging out pucks and getting physical with the other team.

Gross misconduct: A serious infraction that occurs when a player, coach, manager or even trainer purposely violates the rules of the game. The offending individual is suspended for the remainder of the game and is assessed an automatic $200 fine. If a player incurs three game misconduct penalties during the regular season, that player receives an automatic $1000 fine and is suspended for the next league game. In the event of any subsequent game misconduct penalties, the suspension is increased by one game.

Guardian: The goaltender.

G

Hacking: Also known as slashing. An infraction in which a player swings his stick at an opponent, earning a minor penalty.

Handcuffed: When the goaltender has a difficult time stopping an easy-looking shot, he is said to be handcuffed. For example, a goaltender is handcuffed when the puck hits him in the glove, and he can't seem to control the shot.

Handle the puck: To touch or hold onto the puck. If any player other than the goaltender closes his hand on the puck, the referee calls an automatic two-minute minor penalty. A player may, however, grab the puck out of the air, but he must immediately knock the puck down or place it on the ice. If a player knocks an airborne puck toward a teammate, the referee or linesman will call "a pass with the hand," and a face-off is taken in the area of the infraction. However, a hand pass to a teammate while in the defensive zone is permitted.

The goaltender cannot hold on to the puck for longer than three seconds if there is no pressure from the opposing team. If the goaltender does not release the puck after three seconds, a two-minute minor penalty to the goaltender is assessed.

H

Hard around: A hard shot into the offensive zone that follows the boards into the corner, behind the net and then into the opposite corner. The hard around is used to set up offensive plays, particularly power plays.

Hash marks: Often referred to by announcers but seldom explained, the hash marks are a wonderfully colorful way of describing the setup lines within the four faceoff circles. When two players line up within the faceoff circles to the left and right of the goal, there are a series of lines painted on the ice that the players must stand behind before the linesman will drop the puck. If a player crosses the hash mark lines, he can be thrown out of the faceoff and a teammate will have to replace him.

Hat trick: Three goals scored by a player in one game. When the third goal is scored, it is traditional for the fans to throw their hats onto the ice in celebration. This strange ritual dates back many years to one enthusiastic hockey fan and an opportunistic hockey player.

Prior to 1946, when a player scored three goals, it was called a "three-goal game" and fans did not throw anything on the ice. That changed one fateful day, when fashionable Chicago Blackhawks forward Alex Kaleta walked into a Toronto haberdashery owned by Sammy Taft. Kaleta had a game that night against the Leafs and decided to make a bet with the hatmaker and ardent Leafs fan. Kaleta bet the hatter that if he scored three goals in the game that night at Maple Leaf Gardens, Taft would have to give him a hat of his choice for free. Knowing that Kaleta was not the greatest goal scorer in the league and that a three-goal game was difficult to achieve, Taft gladly took the bet from the young Chicago forward. That night, Kaleta scored his three goals against the Leafs and walked into the hat store the next day to collect his winnings.

Newspapers got wind of the story, and Taft was quoted in all the city's major dailies as saying, "Yeah, that was some trick he pulled to get that hat." From that day on, whenever a player scored three goals in one game, it was known as a "hat trick." Never one to pass up a good marketing opportunity when it arose, Taft offered a free hat

H

to every Toronto Maple Leafs player who scored a hat trick in a home game. Eventually, Taft retired from haberdashery, and since then, the fans have picked up where he left off and throw their hats on the ice every time a player pots three goals.

Head butt: When one player hits another with his head. Any player caught head butting receives an automatic match penalty.

Head-man the puck: A term used more often these days with the new rule that has removed the red line at center ice, allowing players to make a two-line pass. When a player head-man's the puck, he quickly passes it up to a player who has sneaked in the back door behind the defensemen. Head-manning the puck is part of the more open, offensive style of hockey that the league has been trying to promote since they tweaked the rules at the start of the 2005–06 season.

Heel of the stick: The part of the stick between the straight part of the shaft and the flat part of the bottom of the blade.

Helmet: A hockey player's head protection. You would think that in a sport as fast and as rough as hockey, the helmet would have been one of the first pieces of equipment to become standard for every player, but it wasn't until 1979 that the NHL passed a rule requiring all players entering the league to wear helmets.

The first helmets made their appearance in the 1930s but were generally scoffed at by players because of their strange appearance. They were usually constructed out of thick, padded leather or a substance called Bakelite (a early type of plastic) and were held in place with an odd leather chinstrap. In the early days of the NHL, players wore helmets only while recovering from an injury. The old "brain bucket" would have served many players well in the early days, as several high-profile players were forced to retire from the game prematurely because of head injuries. Among them was Irvin "Ace" Bailey of the Toronto Maple Leafs, whose career ended when he smacked his head on the ice after receiving a vicious body check from Eddie Shore. Gordie Howe almost lost his life when his head hit the ice hard after he missed a body check.

The first-ever recorded instance of a player wearing a helmet was in 1913, when Moose Johnson of the New Westminster Royals in the Pacific Coast Hockey Association donned a crudely made helmet to protect the broken jaw

H

he had suffered in a game. The last helmet-less player in the National Hockey League was Craig MacTavish, who retired from the game in 1997.

High stick: An infraction in which a player hits an opponent in the neck or face with his stick. The result is usually a two-minute minor penalty, but if blood is drawn, the offending player must sit in the penalty box for four minutes.

Hip check: When a player uses his hip to check an opponent. Because the impact is to the lower part of the body, the person being checked often gets thrown into the air.

Hit the hemp: To score. The "hemp" is the net.

Hockey: The etymology of the name is difficult to trace back to a single source, and there are a number of possible origins for the name of the sport:

- *Hoquet* is an old French word used to describe a shepherd's crook or bent stick. There was also a field game played in France called *hoque*, but there is little evidence that it was ever played in Canada or on ice. *Hoquet* was brought to England with the invasion of William the Conqueror in 1066, and the word gradually evolved into the form and spelling we recognize today.

- As far back as the early 1400s, in England, there is reference to a game called variously *hawkey, hawkie, horkey, hooky, hoky* and *hockey.* It was played during harvest festivals, when young boys got covered in mud playing in the fields with curved sticks and a ball.

- In 1527, in Ireland, there is reference in a book of statutes to a sport that involved "the horlinge of the litill balle with hockie stickes or staves."

- The Middle Dutch word *hokkie*, meaning "shack" or "doghouse," was commonly used to refer to a goal. There are several Dutch paintings from the 16th century that depict people playing a hockey-like game on ice.

The game had many names in the beginning, but it was around the mid-1800s that it became more widely known as hockey. There are several written reports of military men playing hockey in their free time, including one from a British army officer stationed in Kingston, Ontario, in 1843, who wrote in his journal: "Began to skate

H

this year, improved quickly and had great fun at hockey on the ice."

Hockey by any other name: Throughout history, cultures across the globe have played games that in some form or another resemble modern hockey. Below is a list of the many historical and modern variations of hockey:

- **Baddin:** A folk variety of field hockey played in Cheshire, England, in the 19th century.

- **Bandy:** Similar to ice hockey but played on a surface the size of a soccer pitch. This sport is popular in Russia and Scandinavian countries. The National Bandy Association was established in 1891.

- **Cheuca:** A game similar to field hockey played by the Aracuano natives of Argentina.

- **Keretizein:** An ancient Greek game not unlike field hockey, played with crooked sticks and a ball.

- **Khong kangjei:** Also known as "Manipuri hockey" or "wrestling hockey." It is played mainly along the border between India and Burma. Player use sticks similar to hockey sticks to move a ball about a field. Players are allowed to carry the ball, but a goal can only be scored when the ball is hit with a stick. If one player tackles another, the tackled player must submit to a trial of strength, basically a wrestling match. The winner of the match receives possession of the ball.

- **Knattleikr:** An ancient Scandanavian game in which a wooden ball was hit with curved sticks. It may have been played on iced-over fields.

- **Koora (Arab ball):** A type of field hockey played in Algeria near Menea.

- **Melat:** A violent medieval game played in French Brittany with a ball and hard, curved sticks. It was frequently banned by the Church because of the numerous brawls that occured during games.

- **Ringette:** A sport similar to hockey in which players use a stick without a blade and a large ring instead of a puck. It was invented in Canada by Sam Jacks of North Bay, Ontario, in 1963.

- **Roller hockey:** The rules are similar to those of modern ice hockey, but this sport is played on in-line roller skates on a cement surface.

H

- **Underwater hockey:** Not all variations of hockey are played on hard surfaces. Underwater hockey is played on the bottom of a swimming pool. The players use short sticks to move a weighted puck across the bottom of the pool to the opposing team's goal. The game was invented in 1954 in England and was originally called "octopush."

H

Hockey mom/dad: More than just the poor parents who wake up at 4:30 AM to drive their children to the hockey arena, hockey moms and dads are the driving force behind the millions of kids who dream of one day making it into the professional ranks. Hockey moms and dads are there to pick up their kids' spirits when they lose the championship and cheer them on every game from the frigid stands of arenas across North America. Occasionally, the hockey moms' and dads' love for the game and their children leads to the odd scuffle with other hockey parents, but they can be forgiven after having woken up at 4:00 AM every weekend.

Holding: Any action in which a player holds or grabs onto another player and impedes his movement on the ice. The infraction receives a two-minute minor penalty.

Holes (one through seven): There are seven distinct positions that a goaltender needs to cover:

1. At the corner of the net on the ice on the goaltender's stick side

2. At the corner of the net on the ice on the goaltender's glove side

3. On the goaltender's glove side, near the upper crossbar

4. On the goaltender's stick side, near the upper crossbar

5. Between the goaltender's legs. The five-hole is the only hole named by number

6. Between the goaltender's torso and the stick arm

7. Between the goaltender's torso and the glove arm

Hooking: An infraction in which a player uses the blade of his stick to hook another player to slow him down. Under the new, stricter NHL guidelines, contact can be minimal, but as long as the offending player puts his stick around the waist of his opponent, the referee will call

H

a hooking penalty. By far the most common penalty in hockey.

Hot dog: A player who loves to show off his skills and take all the glory for himself.

Hot moment: An old-time hockey term for a fight.

H

Howitzer: Not the classic field artillery cannon used in warfare, but a very hard slapshot. The puck travels so fast that it seems as if it has just come out of a cannon. "Sheldon Souray blasted a howitzer past a surprised goaltender."

Hurley-on-ice: The name for an early version of hockey. The same rules applied as for regular hurling, but the game was played on ice. As the game began to evolve further away from its roots, the name changed.

Hybrid style: A cross between butterfly and stand-up goaltending, hybrid style is not used by many goaltenders these days, but the ones who do use it have found some of the greatest success in the National Hockey League. A hybrid goaltender is adept at dropping to his knees to make a butterfly save and equally capable of making a classic Terry Sawchuk–style kick save.

The hybrid style is one of the most effective
ways of keeping the opposing shooters guessing
whether to shoot the puck high or low. The two
most effective practitioners of this style have
been Martin Brodeur and Dominik Hasek, whose
unpredictability and flare for making big saves
have kept them at the top of the goaltending
world since they broke into the National Hockey
League.

H

I

Ice palace: A hockey arena. Hockey is so important to North American culture that regal names are given to the places where the sport is played. It seems fitting to call the sheet of ice where so many hopes and dreams are played out on a weekly basis, where battles are won and lost, and where legends are made, an ice palace.

Icing the puck: This occurs when a player from a team in its own defensive end shoots the puck the length of the ice, and a player from the other team touches the puck first. The red line is used as the marker for icing. If, for example, a player shoots the puck but has not yet crossed the red line, then the linesman will call icing. Icing is waved off when the goalie or a player on the team that iced the puck touches the puck or when the puck does not make it past the goal line.

Illegal equipment: The NHL has very strict regulations as to the size and fit of players' equipment, and any player who alters equipment to gain advantage is penalized if caught. For example, goaltender Tony Esposito was famous for making alterations to his equipment, including stuffing extra padding into his leg pads and stitching netting under his arms. One of the more common equipment infractions in the NHL is the illegally curved stick, and the most famous incident of a penalty being called on a player was during the 1993 Stanley Cup finals between the Montreal Canadiens and the Los Angeles Kings.

In the second game of the series, the Canadiens were down by one goal in the dying minutes of the third period, when head coach Jacques Demers asked the referee to check the Kings Marty McSorley's stick for an illegal curve. When the referee measured the stick, it was deemed to be illegal and a two-minute penalty was assessed. On the ensuing power play, the Canadiens managed to tie the game and eventually win it in overtime. It was the turning point in the series, and the Canadiens went on to win their 23rd Stanley Cup.

Insurance goal: When a team is already leading the game by one point and scores another goal to take a comfortable lead.

In the slot: The real estate in front of the goal-tender between the faceoff circles. The slot is the place on the ice where every true goal scorer is born—Monopoly's Boardwalk for hockey. Because it is such a sought-after piece of territory, it is the scene of many hockey scrums and fights. If a player can get open in the slot, then he has a direct shot at the goaltender, but if a defenseman is doing his job, then the slot's availability is quickly shut off. With a quick shot and deadly accuracy, Brett Hull was one of the most effective players at finding an opening in the slot and putting the puck in the net.

Interference: An infraction in which one player deliberately obstructs or impedes another who does not have possession of the puck. An interference penalty can also be given if a player drops his stick, glove or helmet and another player knocks it away. A minor penalty is imposed on the offending player.

International ice hockey rink: Every rink outside North America follows International Ice Hockey Federation guidelines when it comes to the size of the playing surface. To increase the speed and the number of goals scored, international rinks are considerably wider than NHL rinks, which are 200 feet by 85 feet. With a playing surface 98 feet wide, players have more space to maneuver and hopefully, for the fans, score more goals.

I

J

Jaw fest: A heated discussion between two players or occasionally two coaches on the bench.

Johnny on the spot: A term for a player who is always in the right place at the right time to slip the puck into an open net.

Juiced: In the world of modern sports, juiced has come to mean two things:

- When a player puts all his power into a shot, he is said to have juiced the puck.

- No longer just the title of Jose Canseco's autobiography, juiced has come to refer to any player who is using drugs (usually steroids) to enhance his performance.

Kept in: When a defending team fails to get the puck out of their own zone, the puck is said to have been "kept in."

Kitchen: The area inside the goaltender's crease or directly in front of the goalie. "The game plan is to get into Dominik Hasek's kitchen."

Kneeing: Considered one of the dirtier penalties in hockey. Hitting an opponent with a knee on knee often leads to the player either being taken out of the game or injured so severely that he is out for the season. A major or misconduct penalty is usually given for kneeing because it is an intentional attempt to injure. Kneeing is considered a cheap shot.

Knuckle puck: One of the most deceptive ways to shoot a puck. The shooter lays the puck on its edge and shoots a wrist shot or slapshot on net. The puck is supposed to flip through the air at a deceptive speed, hopefully confusing the goaltender so that he is unable to stop it. The term is borrowed from baseball's knuckleball.

K

Laser beam: A very hard and accurate shot.

Larceny: When a goaltender makes an impossible save on a shooter, robbing the shooter of his scoring opportunity. The term can also be used when a player jumps into the path of a shooter with an open net and takes away a golden opportunity for a goal. See "robbed."

Laying on the lumber: Also known as slashing. An infraction in which a player swings his stick at an opponent, earning a minor penalty.

Lead pass: When a defender passes the puck up the ice to a streaking forward. Hopefully a lead pass will lead to a fast break or a breakaway on goal.

Left wing lock: A defensive strategy in which the left wing drops back to play parallel to the defense when the other team tries to exit their zone.

Lid: Helmet.

Lie: The angle made by the shaft of the stick and the blade.

Light the lamp: Score a goal. When a goal is scored, the goal judge switches on a red light situated just behind the net. Hector "Toe" Blake of the old Montreal Canadiens scored so many times in his career that he earned the nickname "Old Lamplighter."

Linesman: An assistant to the referee. There are two linesmen on the ice during a game, and it is their job to call infractions such as offsides, icing, high sticks, hand passes and freezing the puck. In rare cases, a linesman can advise the referee of an infraction on the ice if he fails to see it, but it is ultimately the referee that makes the final call. However, a linesman is allowed to assess a bench minor if a player or a member of the coaching staff is verbally abusive. Linesmen are also responsible for most of the faceoffs and usually get to break up scrums and fights.

Loafer: An opportunistic player who loafs or lingers around the neutral zone awaiting a long

L

pass from one of his teammates for a fast break on goal.

Lob: A type of shot used when a player in the defensive zone wants to clear the puck down the ice and avoid icing the puck all the way to the other end. To relieve the pressure in the defensive zone, a player will lift (or lob) the puck over the heads of his opponents, clearing it into the neutral zone and the opposing team's end.

Long bomb: A puck that is slapped on net from far out, sometimes past the blue line or even center ice. It should be an easy save, but sometimes a long bomb can handcuff a goaltender. Every goaltender dreads letting this type of shot into the net.

Loose change: A puck laying on the ice and that nobody can seem to find.

Loose play: A team that plays a game with absolutely no effort or "jump" in their skates— a coach's worst nightmare. When players don't cover their positions and turn over the puck easily, they are said to be playing "loose" hockey.

Lord Stanley's Mug: The Stanley Cup.

Lumber: A hockey stick. Long, long ago, hockey sticks were made of wood or "lumber." Actually, the very first hockey sticks were carved out of a single piece of hardwood.

L

Major penalty: A five-minute penalty that is assessed for a serious violation of the rules. The referee automatically gives a major penalty to an offending player or players when there is a fight or when a minor penalty such as slashing is done with the intent to injure another player.

Man on!: When a player is chasing the puck and has his back to the play, his teammates will yell "Man on!" to let the player know that an opposing player is right on his heels.

Mask: "Real men don't wear masks!" That was the prevailing attitude in the early days of the National Hockey League, though some players were very aware of the need to stay safe. "Your first priority was staying alive," said Glenn Hall, "and your second priority was stopping the puck." Jacques Plante broke the mold in 1959 and began to regularly don a mask during games. But the evolution of the mask did not begin with the Montreal Canadiens goaltender;

it started 29 years earlier with a goaltender named Clint Benedict.

Montreal Maroons goaltender Clint Benedict was the first to break with tradition and wear a mask during regulation game play. He first wore his padded leather mask after receiving a Howie Morenz slapshot directly to the nose and cheekbone. Benedict realized that if he were to sustain another such injury, he might not be able to ever return to the game, so he fashioned himself a mask that covered his forehead, nose, cheeks and mouth. But the crude mask could not protect his face against harder shots, and just a few games later, Benedict was forced to retire after taking another shot to the nose.

Montreal Canadien Jacques Plante was the first NHL goaltender to wear a mask on a regular basis. As the curved stick became the fashion across the league, goaltenders increasingly went down with career-threatening injuries. During a game on November 1, 1959, Plante received a shot from Andy Bathgate directly to the face, and after being stitched up in the dressing room, Plante decided it was time to put on a mask. After that night, he never played

M

without face protection again, despite his coach Toe Blake's hatred of the new contraption.

Over the years, goaltenders have modified and added to the design of the facemask, making for some very interesting looks over the years. The modern face mask is set off the face by protective padding, with angled lines to deflect the energy of a direct hit by the puck, and has a built-in cage that protects the eyes while still allowing the player to see the puck.

The last goaltender to go without wearing a face mask in a game was Andy Brown of the Pittsburgh Penguins. He played without a mask for the final time on April 7, 1974, in a game against the Atlanta Flames.

M

Match penalty: The most serious type of penalty. An automatic ejection from the game is given to any player who attempts to injure or deliberately injures another player, with the added punishment of a five-minute penalty to be served by another member of the team.

Minor hockey: From as early as five years of age, kids can enter into the North American hockey system. As they get older and their skills improve, they move through the various levels in the

system. Not all the levels are age restricted.
If a child is bigger than others his or her age or
is a far better player, then he or she is moved
up to the higher levels. Sidney Crosby entered
the professional National Hockey League at
18 years of age.

- **Tyke, Mite or Squirt:** Ages 5–6; kids learn
  the basics of the game

- **Novice:** Ages 7–8; emphasis is on moving
  away from pack-style hockey

- **Atom:** Ages 9–10

- **PeeWee:** Ages 11–12

- **Bantam:** Ages 13–14

- **Midget:** Ages 15–17

- **Juvenile or Junior:** Ages 18–20

Minor penalty: A penalty of two minutes is
assessed for offenses such as hooking, tripping, elbowing and cross-checking. During the
two-minute penalty, the offending player sits
out his sentence in the penalty box and can
only return when the two minutes are over or
the opposing team scores a goal.

Misconduct penalty: A penalty assessed for a serious infraction, such as when a player uses abusive language towards the officials or does not obey the referee's requests. The referee indicates a misconduct penalty by placing both hands on his hips. In the event of a misconduct penalty, the player is removed from the ice for a period of 10 minutes, and a substitute player is permitted to replace the penalized player. The offending player is also assessed an automatic fine of $100.

Mouse: What you get under your eye when you take a good elbow.

Mucker: A player who is known for causing trouble and getting involved in disputes with the officials.

Mucking: Interfering with another player. "The player received a two-minute penalty for mucking around with the goaltender."

Nail-biter: A close game.

Natural hat trick: When a player scores three goals in a row without any other player on either team scoring during his run. It is a rare occurrence in professional hockey.

Net: The goal. The first hockey goals did not have nets and were simply two objects (usually rocks) spaced evenly apart to demarcate the area of the goal. During the 1800s, cricket terminology once again found its way into the new game as the "goalposts" became known as "rickets." As the game evolved, two metal poles took the place of rocks as goal line markers. Since it was difficult to decide whether or not a goal had been scored, goals were judged by an umpire who stood directly behind the goal. The goal umpire would stand slightly behind the net dressed in heavy winter attire, and whenever a goal was scored, he would ring a loud brass bell. Depending on the affiliations of the goal judges, not all their decisions could be trusted, so another alternative had to be found to appease all parties.

Fishing nets were first attached to the metal posts in the late 1890s to make the job of the goal judge easier, but it wasn't until 1912 that one innovative goaltending legend invented the modern hockey net.

Percy LeSueur had long been a student of the game, and he was always looking for ways to improve it. In 1912, he made a few modifications to the nets used at the time, most notably the addition of a crossbar, giving the hockey net the basic shape that is still used today.

N

Netminder: A goaltender.

Neutral zone: The area between the blue lines. It is designated the neutral zone because it is in neither the offensive nor the defensive zone.

O

Offensive zone: Also known as the attacking zone. The area of the ice in which one team is on the defense and the other is on the offense looking to score.

Office: The area behind the net. This colorful term was popularized by the play of Wayne Gretzky. As a player, Gretzky spent most of his time in the offensive zone behind the opposing team's net because it gave him protection from the defensemen and a good vantage point from which to survey the ice. He spent so much of his ice time behind the net racking up assists that the area became known as his office.

"I started when I was in Junior B," said Gretzky in Andrew Podniek's book *The Great One.* "I was too small—5'5", 110 pounds—to stay in front of the goal, so Gene Popeil, my coach, told me to stake out some space for myself behind it and stay off to one side." If a defenseman was sent in after Gretzky, he could either pass the puck to a teammate in front or quickly move to the other side of the "office" and keep everybody guessing as to what his next move might be. Few other players in NHL history have used the office as effectively as the Great One.

Off-ice officials: Also known as minor officials. These officials are not positioned on the ice but play an important role in assisting the referee and linesmen. They include the official scorer, game timekeeper, penalty timekeeper and judges. In the era of video replay, the off-ice officials have become almost as important as the ones on the ice.

Offside: The offside defines the legal or illegal position of a player and the puck on the ice. It is used to keep one team from gaining an advantage over the other team. An offside occurs when a player or players cross the opposing team's blue line ahead of the puck. A player's stick can cross the line ahead of the puck, even one skate, but if the player's entire body crosses the blue line, then the linesman will call an offside and set up for a faceoff. Prior to 2004, an offside also occurred when a player in his own defensive zone passed the puck to a teammate who had crossed the center red line—commonly called a two-line pass—but in order to promote a more offensive game, the NHL removed the red line from the offside equation.

O

Onside: A player is onside if he does not cross the opposing team's blue line ahead of the puck. The linesman will usually signal a close onside call by waving his arms to the side, called a "wash out," indicating to the players that the play was not offside.

On the train tracks: When a player is lined up to get body checked by an oncoming player.

One-timer: An effective way of getting the puck into the net. A one-timer occurs when a player passes the puck to an open teammate, and the teammate takes a shot immediately without stopping the puck. A one-timer is most often used during a power play. Defensemen score a lot of goals in this manner.

O

Open wing: A part of the ice where a player expects his teammate to be, but the teammate has either neglected his duties or been caught out of position and cannot receive the pass.

Outlet pass: A pass from behind the blue line to a streaking forward heading through the neutral zone.

Overtime: During the regular season, if two teams fail to break a tie after three periods of play, they enter into a five-minute overtime period.

Paddle down: When the goaltender puts the widest part of his stick along the ice, usually when an opponent is coming out from the corner or from behind the net. With the goaltender committed to protecting the lower half of the net, the shooter can lift the puck into the upper part of the goal, but because the paddle down technique is only used when the shooter is in close, it is difficult to get the puck over the goalie.

Paint: The blue-colored goal crease.

Penalty box: Also called the "sin bin." The area directly off the ice where players serve out their penalty minutes.

Penalty killing: When one team goes on the power play, the other team must kill the penalty. The players on the PK (penalty kill) have the difficult job of protecting their defensive zone while missing one or two players.

P

Penalty shot: A free shot that is awarded when a player who has a clear path towards the goal is pulled down from behind or hooked, or if a stick is thrown. Often called the most exciting play in hockey, a penalty shot does not happen often, but when it does, it is certain to get the crowd on its feet. When a penalty shot is awarded, the referee places the puck at center ice and the player is allowed to skate in on the goalie for a free shot. The player must be in continuous forward motion with the puck, and once the shot is taken, the player cannot take a second shot in the event of a rebound. Once the puck is immobilized, it is considered dead.

When the penalty shot rule was first introduced into the National Hockey League for the 1934–35 season, a player could not move in on the goaltender as is practiced today, but rather he had to stand behind a line 28 feet from the goal and take his shot. Not the easiest of tasks, but one player managed to score in the penalty shot's first years of existence. The first-ever penalty shot was awarded to Montreal Canadien Armand Mondou on November 10, 1934, and he was stopped by Toronto Maple Leafs goaltender Georges Hainsworth. Just three days later, Ralph "Scotty" Bowman of the St. Louis Eagles scored

P

the first penalty shot goal in NHL history on Montreal Maroons goaltender Alex Connell.

During the 1941–42 NHL season, the league introduced two types of penalty shots, classed as major and minor. The minor penalty shot was taken from a line 28 feet from the goal and awarded when a player had been only slightly interfered with on a break to the net. A major penalty shot was given to a player who was tripped up from behind on a break. The major penalty shot allowed the player to skate in on the goaltender to shoot or fake from any distance. Eventually the minor penalty shot was discontinued, and the NHL was left with the penalty shot that remains to the present day.

On June 5, 2006, Edmonton Oiler Chris Pronger became the first player in the history of the NHL to score on a penalty shot in the Stanley Cup finals.

Picking his pocket: When an unsuspecting player moves up the ice with the puck and another player moves in from behind and steals the puck from him, the first player's pocket is said to have been picked.

Pillows: A goalie's pads.

Playoff beard: A long-standing tradition or superstition in which players grow their beards during their team's entire playoff run to the Stanley Cup and only shave them off once their team has been eliminated or wins the Cup.

Playoffs: After a long regular season, teams who qualify make it into the playoffs. The playoffs are a sequence of rounds in which teams are gradually eliminated until a single team is left as the Stanley Cup champion.

Plumber: A third- or fourth-line player who can't score.

Plus-minus: A player receives a "plus" if he is on the ice when his team scores an even-strength or shorthanded goal. He receives a "minus" if he is on the ice for an even-strength or shorthanded goal scored by the opposing club. The difference in these numbers is considered that player's plus-minus statistic.

P

Poke check: A technique employed by the goaltender that is intended to poke or push the puck off an opponent's stick as he comes in close to the net. In making the play for the puck, the goaltender slides his hand up the shaft of his stick and makes a stab at the player's stick. This is usually a dangerous move for a goaltender, because if he misses the poke check, he is left to the mercy of the shooter. Two of the earliest goaltenders to employ this strategy with success were Jacques Plante of the Montreal Canadiens and Johnny Bower of the Toronto Maple Leafs.

Point: Used in reference to the defensemen when hockey was played by a team of seven players on the ice. The point position was similar to that of the modern-day defenseman. While defensemen in the six-player game play side by side, the point position player was set up behind the cover point directly in front of the goal-keeper. The point player usually remained in the defensive zone while the forwards took the puck up the ice. As a result, the point player hardly ever scored.

Point-blank range: A shot from directly in front of the net.

Policeman: A player who is the protector on the team. See "enforcer."

Pond hockey: Hockey played on a small, frozen body of water. The local pond is where the game of hockey really began. Long before local munici-palities put up rinks and way before indoor

P

arenas were common, the game was, and still is, played outside on the local pond. Played without a goaltender, players usually shoot the puck into a net as wide as a regular goal but only a few inches off the ground. This does not allow for slapshots in the game, placing emphasis on players' skating abilities.

Post-to-post save: When a goaltender has to make a save at one side of the net and then dive to the other side to make another save.

Pot a goal: To score.

Power forward: An above-average-sized player who can be physically imposing in the corners and in front of the net. Not just a physical presence on the ice, the power forward is one of the most sought-after players to have on a team.

P

Power play (PP): When a player on one team is penalized, the opposing team goes on the power play. They have the advantage of having all their players still on the ice while the penalized team must play shorthanded for two minutes or more. A coach will normally send out his most offensive players on the power play to take advantage of the situation.

Puck: The black, vulcanized rubber disc used to score goals—probably the most essential piece of equipment in the game of hockey. National Hockey League regulations say that the puck must be one inch thick, 3 inches in diameter and weigh between 5.5 and 6 ounces. Since a warm puck bounces more, game pucks are kept on ice throughout the game.

The little black disc has had a strange and unique evolution. The word "puck" has its origins in Middle English and refers to a mischievous sprite in folklore (most famously depicted in William Shakespeare's *A Midsummer Night's Dream*). The modern definition of the word comes from ice hockey's close relative, hurling. When a hurling player hit the ball, he was said to "puck it." This term got carried over to ice hockey, where players constantly hit or "pucked" the ball about. So when the hurling ball no longer suited the needs of ice hockey, players substituted a flat wooden disc, which they in turn dubbed a puck.

It is hard to imagine hockey players using anything besides the little vulcanized rubber pucks that we have today, but in the early days of the game, players made pucks out of wood from trees that surrounded the outdoor rinks. Cherrywood

P

was the wood of choice for the discerning puck connoisseur, because the bark stuck to the wood well, making the puck visible on the white of the ice and snow. As the game became more organized and players got faster, they began to search out other materials to use for pucks. Wood was very light, making the disc hard to control when shooting, and after a few good smacks with the sticks, the bark began to break off. The solution was to replace wood with rubber. But the first rubber pucks were not as solidly constructed as they are today. The earliest ones were made up of several layers of rubber cemented together. The puck was heavier and easier to shoot, but there was a problem—if the cement did not hold, the puck would often split into several different pieces. This proved to be a real problem during several early professional games.

In 1900, during a game in Belleville, Ontario, that was refereed by legendary official Fred Waghorne, a player released a hard shot on goal that hit the goalpost and split the puck in two pieces. One half bounced into the corner of the ice and the other half of the puck ended up in the net. An immediate controversy arose as one team claimed it was a goal, while the opposing team demanded that it be disallowed. Referee Fred Waghorne immediately pulled out his rule book and pointed to the section that said an official puck must be one inch thick. Since the puck in the net was not regulation size, the goal was disallowed.

In an NHL game, pucks often fly into the crowd or are taken by a rookie who has just scored his first goal, which is why there are dozens of pucks waiting on the sidelines if they are needed. Amazingly enough, on November 10, 1979, in a game between the Los Angeles Kings and the Minnesota North Stars, only one puck was used for the entire match.

Puck bunny: A not-so-flattering reference to a woman who hovers around hockey players. Used generally as a reference to women who are only out for sexual encounters with players rather than for the love of the game. The term is analogous to the word "groupie" as it relates to music and celebrity.

Puck has eyes: A phrase that describes when a player shoots the puck through traffic, and it somehow finds its way to the back of the net as if it had eyes and was able to avoid the mess of bodies in front of the net.

Puck hog: A player who holds onto the puck for a long time, looking to make the play by himself, without any help from his teammates. Not often used to describe a professional player, it is more often used to refer to a minor league player or weekend warrior who thinks he is a professional.

Puck luck: A serendipity puck. For example, one that hits the crossbar of the net instead of going in. This is puck luck for the defending team.

Pucksters: A colloquial term for people who play hockey. "I was down at the pond with the local pucksters all day."

Punch up: A fight.

Pylon: A player who is not a very good skater, and who is easy to skate around.

P

Quarrel: A fight.

Questionable call: When a referee calls a penalty that in the eyes of the offending player and the team should not have been called.

Quick up: A quick pass up the ice.

Q

R

Ragging: Clever stickhandling by a team to keep the puck away from the opposition and kill a penalty.

Rear guard: A defenseman.

Rebound: When a shot hits the goaltender, usually on the leg pads, and bounces out. Rebounds are dangerous for a goaltender because they often bounce out to the wrong player, leaving the goalie out of position or with an open net. When that happens, it is referred to as a "juicy rebound."

Red-light district: The area immediately in front of the net where most of the shots on goal come from.

Referee: Ever since hockey changed from an afternoon pastime to a competitive match, there have been referees to ensure that the game is played according to the rules of combat. It is the referee's job to signal penalties, and he is the only person on the ice who can signal a goal. Referees generally shy away from breaking up fights, instead remaining at a distance ready to hand out penalties for a sucker punch or elbow that might be missed if he was busy breaking up two players. Because referees often call penalties that change the outcome of a game, they are not always the best-liked people in hockey, whether in the 1800s or the 21st century. In 1895, after an Ottawa-Quebec game, two officials had to be rescued by police when a mob of irate Quebec fans dragged them to the back of the arena and tried to "convince" them to change Ottawa's 3–2 victory to a draw. In a 1903 Stanley Cup game between the Ottawa Silver Seven and the Rat Portage Thistles, the game became so violent that the referee had to wear a hard hat to protect himself from flying sticks and the debris launched by fans.

The modern NHL referee can be distinguished by his black-and-white-striped uniform with orange armbands—a far cry from the first referees, who dressed in heavy coats, boots, scarves and derby hats to protect themselves from the cold outdoor conditions. Over the years, hockey and the rules that govern it have changed, but the role of the referee has remained

R

the same—to ensure that the rules are followed and to keep the game fair and entertaining.

Referee's crease: An area directly in front of the timekeeper's bench marked on the ice by a red line. A player can be penalized for pursuing a referee into his crease to argue a call. It serves no function during play.

Ricket: A cricket term that defines the goal. There is evidence that all kinds of games were adapted to the icy conditions of Canadian winters, with cricket being one of them. The term "rickets" was also used to refer to the goalposts in the early days of hockey.

Ricochet: When the puck bounces off another player and goes into the net, giving the goaltender absolutely no chance to stop the puck. A goaltender will usually give his defensemen an exasperated look and shrug his shoulders, as there is nothing they could have done on the shot.

R

Riding the pine: The players' bench, "the pine," is the domain of the backup goaltender (ask Martin Brodeur's backup, Scott Clemmensen), who sits on the bench more than he plays between the pipes. "After riding the pine for five games, he finally gets the start for tonight's big matchup."

Right in the numbers: To cross-check a player in the back (where his number is), close to the boards, usually resulting in a penalty.

Ring it off Irene: Not often used and probably invented by a television sportscaster to liven up a broadcast, this phrase simply means that the puck has hit the goalpost.

Ring it off the iron: When a player fires a hard shot off the goalpost, and it makes a distinctive "ping" sound.

Rink: Normally defined as an expanse of ice designated for ice skating or hockey, or an area marked off for a sport to be played. "Let's go play hockey at the rink." Most people know what a rink is, but this odd-sounding word has its roots in a more violent and bloody time, which seems to mesh well with the physical nature of the game of hockey. The term originates from the Middle Ages from both Scottish and French words:

- *Renk*, a Scottish word that means "an area designed for a battle, joust or race"

- *Renc*, an Old French word for "racecourse"

R

The modern word "rink" most likely evolved from the Scottish *renc*, since throughout the history of hockey, the play on the ice has often resembled a medieval battle, except that today's modern rink warrior brandishes a hockey stick instead of a sword and shoulder pads instead of armor.

The modern-day North American hockey rink is rectangular, with rounded corners surrounded by wooden or fiberglass boards about four feet in height. The standard size as determined by the National Hockey League is 200 feet by 85 feet with a corner radius of 28 feet. The distance between the goal line and the end boards is set at 11 feet. The distance from the goal line out to the blue line measures 64 feet. The distance between the blue lines, known as the neutral zone, is 50 feet.

R

Other areas of note on the hockey rink are the two faceoff circles found to the left and right of the net. The referee holds the faceoff at the center of the circle.

For the start of the 2005–06 season, the National Hockey League changed a few of the traditional areas on the ice to speed up the game. The most notable change was the area behind the goal line. A trapezoid-shaped area has been marked where the goaltenders are no longer allowed to play the puck. If they do so, they receive a two-minute minor penalty. The rule was put into place to stop puck-handling goaltenders such as Martin Brodeur from acting like a third defense-man, able to pass the puck up to a forward in the hope of starting a fast break.

Rink rat: A young player who scurries around the arena taking every chance he or she can get to be near hockey and to play hockey. Home-work and social life come second for the rink rat.

Ripple the mesh: This happens when a hard shot hits the back of the goal and shakes the netting.

Road apples: Long before the invention of the rubber puck, local children often had to use things that could be readily found around them if they wanted to play hockey. Often, the most readily available source of hockey puck substi-tutes was frozen horse droppings. "Road apples," as they were so charmingly called, worked well for light wrist shots but would break up under the pressure of a slapshot, which would send a piece of "apple" flying into the face of the poor player who was standing in the goal.

R

Rob (of a goal): The act by which a goaltender makes a incredible save, effectively robbing a player of a goal. "Crosby was robbed of a goal as Brodeur jumped across the crease to make a miraculous glove save!"

Roof: The top of the net between the front crossbar and the back of the goal. When a player blasts the puck into the upper part of the net, he has "roofed" the puck.

Roster: A list of players on a team.

Roughing: A penalty given to a player who goes above and beyond the basic physical nature of the game and attempts to injure an opposing player. Referees will usually assess a two-minute penalty for a minor infraction.

When looking back to old-time hockey, many people see those days through rose-colored glasses as a time when gentlemen played the game and fun was had by all with few instances of violence, but early hockey was anything but gentlemanly, and rough play was common.

R

Rover: The rover was a position that was used in the early days of the game and was often referred to as the fourth forward. The rover could venture anywhere on the ice and could be either a defensive or offensive player. On a faceoff, the rover would be positioned directly to the left of the centerman. Because the rover was useful at both ends of the ice, he was usually required to be a fast and highly skilled skater. Lester Patrick, Si Griffis, Hobey Baker and Frank McGee were some of the greatest athletes to ever play the rover position.

The position was officially discontinued when the National Hockey League came into existence in 1917, though other leagues such as the Pacific Coast Hockey Association continued to use it until the 1920s.

Rubber: A puck. During practice, a coach will often say, "All right, let's get the rubber out," meaning that he wants the pucks on the ice so that practice can start.

R

S

Sandwich session: The second period of a hockey game.

Saucer pass: A pass that seems to float slightly above the ice and lands directly on the stick of the receiving player.

Sauve les meubles!: A colorful French term used to describe an incredible play by a goaltender or player to make a save. The literal translation means "Save the furniture!"

Scramble: When the puck is loose in front of the net and players from both teams try to get possession. In the midst of the mayhem, players attempt to get control of the puck to either shoot it into the net or clear it away. You may hear announcers say, "There is a mad scramble in front of the net. The goalie is down and can't find the puck!"

Screen (the goaltender): Sometimes the easiest way to get a puck past a goaltender is to make sure he cannot see it. To screen the goaltender, a shooter will either position himself between the opponent's defensemen or have one of his own teammates stand in front of the goaltender to obstruct the goalie's view of the puck.

Scribe: A hockey writer.

Set play: A strategy or play that a team has practiced so it pays off in games.

Shin pads: In early hockey, the first and most obvious body part the players protected was the shins. The shinbone was often the victim of an errant stick or puck, so players strapped on small leather pads that protected the leg from the skate boot to just below the knee. The type of protection often used before leather pads were invented was anything a player could get his hands on. This meant that players used catalogs, books and newspapers to protect their shins. Modern-day shin pads are light, protect both the shinbone and the knee, and can withstand some of the most powerful slapshots in the NHL.

S

Shinny hockey: There are many definitions for shinny hockey. The word "shinny" comes from the Scottish game of shinty, which was brought to Canada by Scottish immigrants and is a cousin of modern-day hockey. Shinty is a game much like field hockey and was adapted to be played on ice. Although hockey became the dominant game, the term shinny is still used to describe an informal game of hockey. There are no formal rules, but since players have no equipment, the puck cannot be lifted off the ice. The game can be played on ice or concrete.

Shinny can also refer to a game played on one's knees with miniature sticks and a soft ball. Because players are on their knees, the game is usually played in a small room to keep the ball inbounds.

Shootout: A new format implemented by the NHL at the start of the 2005–06 season to break ties at the end of a four-on-four, five-minute overtime after a tie in regulation play. Each team chooses three skaters to take penalty shots on the opposing goaltender. When the three shooters have finished, the team with the most goals wins. If the score remains tied after three shooters, it goes into sudden death, in which each team calls upon one shooter at a time. The first team to score after an opponent's miss wins the game and earns two points. The team that loses the shootout receives one point.

Shorthanded: When one team receives a penalty and is down one or two players, it is said to be shorthanded.

Short side: The side of the goal closest to the shooter.

Shoulder deke: A move used to fake out an opponent in which the attacker makes a quick move of the shoulders one way while moving his body in the other direction.

Shoulder pads: Remarkably, shoulder pads did not appear in professional hockey until the 1930s and at first were disliked by most players. The pads provided little protection, and players found that the pads restricted their movement on the ice. Many players went without shoulder pads into the late 1930s. Modern-day equipment is constructed with hard plastic outer shell, and dense foam underneath absorbs the shock of a body check into the boards.

S

Shutout: When a goaltender stops every shot directed at him during the game. Terry Sawchuk owns the record for the most career shutouts at 103. Georges Hainsworth of the Montreal Canadiens, who compiled an amazing 22 shutouts during the 1928–29 NHL season, holds the record for the most shutouts in one season.

Sieve: A goaltender who lets in a bunch of goals—not a name a goaltender likes having attached to his style of play. A goaltender is branded a sieve because the puck always seems to be able to find a hole through him.

Sin bin: The penalty box.

Slashing: When a player swings his stick at an opponent. Under the old definition, contact was necessary for the infraction to be penalized, but under the new NHL rules, the intent to slash can earn the player a minor penalty. Slashing is also known as "hacking" and "laying on the lumber."

Players known for slashing include Ron Hextall, who received a 12-game suspension for slashing and attacking Montreal Canadien Chris Chelios in game six of the 1989 Stanley Cup playoffs, and Billy Smith, who was well known for slashing the feet of any opposing player who went near his net.

One of the most famous slashing incidents happened when Boston Bruin Marty McSorley slashed Vancouver Canuck Donald Brashear in

S

the head from behind in the 1999–2000 season.
McSorley was suspended from the NHL for one
year and was found guilty of assault with a
weapon in a Vancouver courtroom.

Sleeper: An attacking player who slips into the
center or neutral zone behind the attacking
defensemen.

Slewfoot: Dragging a skate to trip a player.

Soft dump: Not what you think. A soft, lofted
shot (see "dump-in") to the corner. This shot was
inspired by goaltenders such as Marty Brodeur,
who are so good with their sticks that a normal
dump-in has little chance of working.

Slot, in the: An opportunity for a player to score
all alone close to the net.

Slow whistle: When a referee or linesman waits
to blow his whistle because of a delayed penalty
or delayed offside.

Slush: What they called the ice in the old Dallas
Reunion Arena.

Sniper: The most dangerous offensive player
on the ice. A sniper is able to find openings in
the net where others see nothing. If a goaltender

moves out to cut down the angle, leaving only a few inches of open net, the sniper is often able to snap the puck quickly to that open part of the net. Snipers possess a blistering slapshot, a quick release and are always deadly accurate. Alexander Ovechkin and Ilya Kovalchuck are two of the deadliest modern-day snipers in the NHL.

Snow job: Remember when the local bully would plant your face in a snowbank and you'd come up with a beard of snow? Well, goaltenders across the league relive some painful childhood memories every time players stop in front of the crease and send up a wall of white ice in their faces. The snow job is annoying, but it is unfortunately an unavoidable part of the game. Goaltenders spend a lot of time on their knees, and it is a consequence of this position that players charging to the net must come to a complete stop rather abruptly, sending up a spray of ice into the goaltender's face. However, sometimes players purposely snow job the goaltender. A smart goaltender keeps his head down after making a save.

Snow plow: See "snow job."

Soft hands: The innate ability that some players have to handle the puck, making very difficult moves look easy. Players such as Alex Kovalev, Sidney Crosby and Vincent Lecavalier are among the players with the softest hands in the NHL today.

Spearing: Stabbing an opponent with the blade of the stick. An automatic major penalty and game misconduct are given to any player caught spearing an opponent. A player who spears an opponent but does not make contact earns a double minor penalty.

Spin-o-rama: When a player makes one or a series of circles or spins while keeping the puck under control to elude his opponents. The term was invented by broadcasting legend Danny Gallivan and popularized by Denis Savard. This maneuver is especially impressive when the player gets a shot off while performing the spin-o-rama.

Spit splinters: What you do after you get a high stick in the mouth.

S

Split the defense: When a lone player stick-handles the puck between two pinching defensemen, gets through unscathed and goes on to score a goal. Mario Lemieux was one of the best players at splitting the defense, and the time he skated between two Minnesota North Star players to score a goal is still replayed on sports channels as one of the top goals of all time.

Splits: When a goaltender spreads his legs as far as possible in opposite directions to cover the net. Female goaltenders have a much easier time with this one. Used mostly in desperation when the goaltender is caught out of position.

Spread eagle: Another way of describing the butterfly style of goaltending. The goaltender spreads his legs along the goal line, taking away the lower half of the net from the shooter.

Stacking the pads: Generally a move of desperation by a goaltender. When there is a sudden two-on-one break, the goaltender is forced to face the puck carrier, while the lone defenseman tries to block the pass across to the player coming down the opposite side. If the player is able to pass the puck off to his teammate, the goaltender must make a desperate slide across the goal to make the save. One way to do this is by sliding feet-first with the pads stacked on top of each other in the direction of the shooter in an attempt to block as much of the open net as possible.

Stand on his head: An expression used when a goalie makes an exceptional attempt to stop a puck. Whether this has literally ever been accomplished is unlikely, but many goaltenders have come remarkably close to standing on their heads to make a save. Radio and television personalities love to use this colorful expression to describe an acrobatic save, but few know where the actual expression comes from.

Prior to 1918, goaltenders were not allowed to fall to the ice to stop the puck, and if they did, they received a two-minute penalty for the infraction. A goaltender named Clint Benedict did everything in his power to get around this rule and have it overturned. To advance his cause, Benedict developed the unique ability to lose his balance and fall to the ice at the exact moment he needed to make a save. Referees had a difficult time deciding whether Benedict was just weak in the knees or if he was intentionally breaking the rules. For his antics, critics gave Benedict colorful nicknames such as "Praying Benny" and "Tumbling Clint" because he spent so much time on the ice. But Benedict's persistence finally paid off when frustrated referees complained to National Hockey League president Frank Calder. Angered by the referees'

S

inability to call the penalties and worried that other goaltenders might pick up Benedict's bad habits, Calder capitulated and changed the rule on January 9, 1918, allowing goaltenders to fall to the ice to make saves. Obviously annoyed at having his hand forced, Calder stated after changing the rule: "In the future, they can fall on their knees or stand on their heads if they think they can stop the puck better in that way than by standing on their feet."

Stand-up style: In this style of goaltending, the netminder stops the puck while remaining upright. Goalies in the early days of the game were required to use the stand-up style of goaltending simply because they were not allowed to fall to the ice to stop the puck. Thanks to Clint Benedict (see "stand on his head," above), the rule was changed in 1918 to allow goaltenders to fall to their knees to make saves, but the stand-up style continued among the professional ranks for decades, because without the protection of facemasks, goaltenders were still at the mercy of every errant puck and stick that came their way. Goaltenders using this style relied on their quick reflexes to stop pucks that skirted along the ice with a kick save or with their sticks. Even with the advent of the butterfly style of goaltending in the 1960s and with the added protection of modern facemasks, stand-up goaltending remained popular with netminders well into the late 1980s. One of the last proponents of the style was Kirk McLean, who retired from the game in 2001. Some of the most notable goaltenders to use the stand-up style with success were Jacques Plante, Terry Sawchuk, Ken Dryden, Johnny Bower, Bernie Parent and Bill Durnan.

Stanley Cup: The Holy Grail of hockey. Lord Stanley, Governor General of the Dominion of Canada, donated sports' most recognized trophy to the game he loved in 1893. Originally inscribed as the Dominion Hockey Challenge Cup, it was awarded to the top team in amateur hockey and quickly became the most coveted prize in the sport. The first team to win Lord Stanley's Mug (as the Cup is sometimes called) was the Montreal Amateur Athletic Association (AAAs), who took home the trophy in 1893. The Montreal Canadiens have won the most Stanley Cup championships, with 24 wins, followed by the Toronto Maple Leafs, with 13.

Stanza: A period in a hockey game.

S

Starting the wrong lineup: Probably the rarest penalty given in the National Hockey League. Prior to the start of the game, a coach is required to provide a list of the players that will be in the starting lineup to the referee or the official scorer, and if any changes are made to that lineup before the game begins, a bench minor penalty is given to the offending team, provided the referee is notified of the infraction before a second faceoff.

Stay-at-home defenseman: Often referred to as a defenseman's defenseman. The stay-at-home defenseman is a reliable position player who is strongly committed to defense and rarely makes an offensive rush. This type of defenseman scores very few goals but is the best player to put on during a penalty-killing situation.

Stick: The hockey stick has come a long way from its earliest incarnation, which resembled a field hockey stick, to today's modern composite $300 stick. Most people look at a hockey stick and see a simple piece of wood that has been bent into shape. Equipment in the first several decades of the sport remained fairly simple and utilitarian. Hockey sticks were the same sticks the players used in their summer games of hurling, but as the sport evolved, so did the

S

sticks. They lost the extreme curve at the blade, which became flatter so that more surface area would come into contact with the puck.

In 1850, a man named Alexander Rutherford of Lindsay, Ontario, carved a hockey stick out of a tree branch. One hundred and fifty years later, his great-great-grandson had the stick evaluated as the oldest hockey stick in the world. Its appraised value was $2 million.

By the early 1890s, several companies were producing hockey sticks for players across Canada and the northern United States, though many players still made their own sticks in those days from a single piece of yellow birch or hornbeam. The two most popular brands were the Mic-Mac hockey stick and the Rex hockey stick from the Starr Company. In the 1904 edition of the Eaton's catalog, the Mic-Mac brand of stick sold for 39 cents.

S

In the early days of hockey, it was not uncommon for players to call their sticks "hockeys."

Up until the middle of the 20th century, hockey sticks were constructed with relatively the same technology, but by the 1960s, several companies had begun to experiment with fiberglass.

By placing the strong material within the shaft and the blade, sticks lasted much longer and were less likely to break under the rigors of the professional game.

Stone a shooter: To stone a shooter is not to throw rocks at him, but rather it is a goaltender making a spectacular save on a player from in close. The shooter usually finds himself alone in front of the net with the puck, and just as he is about to put it in the open part of the net, the goaltender sticks out a pad, glove or body part to stop the puck and stone the shooter.

Stone hands: A player with few or poor puck-handling skills is said to have stone hands. It can also refer to a player with a really poor shot.

Strip (the puck): To take the puck away from another player. When one player loses the puck to an opponent, he has been stripped of the puck.

Sudden death: A colorful term that describes the overtime or shootout period in hockey. In soccer, an overtime period continues after a team has scored to break a tie, giving the opposition a chance to get back in the game until the time runs out. With just one goal needed to clinch a win for either team in hockey, it is fitting that the overtime period has become known as sudden death. The game ends as soon as the tie-breaking goal is scored, and the opposing team does not get another chance to tie the game.

The term "sudden death" can also be used for the shootout. If the first three shooters do not break the tie, the game comes down to the sudden death shootout in which the first team to finish one round with a goal wins the game.

Sunburn: What a goaltender gets from the red lights behind the net when he lets in a lot of goals.

Superstition: A big factor for many players. For example, many players do not shave during the playoffs, believing that this will improve their chances of winning the Stanley Cup. Other superstitions include always putting on their equipment in the same order, eating the same meal before every game or not showering after a win. Goaltenders are considered to be the most superstitious. Ron Hextall used to smack his stick on the goalpost throughout the game to keep himself focused, Patrick Roy would talk to his goalposts, and Glen Hall had the strange ritual of throwing up before every game.

S

T

Take the man: When a player plays a one-on-one defense against an attacking opponent.

Tape to tape: An accurate pass in which the puck leaves one player's stick blade and hits a teammate's blade directly on the tape.

Tee up the puck: When a player receives a pass, makes sure it is in position for a shot and lets go a cannon of a shot.

Telescope: A way for the goaltender to move forward and backward within his crease without his skates ever leaving the ice. This move is accomplished simply by bringing the feet together to slide backward and separating the feet to move forward. In a game, the goaltender will telescope to get into the right position to face the shooter, usually when the opposing team crosses into the zone.

Texas hat trick: Four goals scored by a player in a single game.

Tic-tac-toe: A fancy play in which an attacking team makes several quick, accurate passes before getting a final shot on net. A tic-tac-toe looks much better if it ends in a goal, of course.

Tickle the twine: When a goal is scored and the puck hits the netting.

Timeout: A timeout is taken when a coach sees that his team needs a break and wants to go over strategy for the next play. It is normally used near the end of a game when a team is down by a goal and is in the attacking zone.

Three stars: A tradition in which the best three players of the game are chosen by the press, the stadium announcers or special invited guests. A hometown player who is selected as one of the three stars skates out onto the ice after the game and salutes the crowd. When a player from the away team is selected, the home crowd usually boos him severely, if he has the nerve to skate out onto the ice.

T

When Montreal Canadiens legend Maurice Richard scored all five goals in a Stanley Cup game against the Toronto Maple Leafs in 1944, he received all three stars for the night. That has never happened to any other player in NHL history since.

Tools of ignorance: A goaltender's equipment.

Too many men on the ice: A frustrating penalty that occurs when a team on a line change leaves too many players on the ice. The regulations state that there can be too many players on the ice as long as those leaving the ice are within five feet of the bench and do not get involved in the play. A two-minute minor is assessed to the offending team.

Traffic: As annoying as the five o'clock rush hour can be, goaltenders hate it just as much when they find a traffic jam of large hockey players in front of their net. If one of the better goaltenders in the league is in goal, the opposing team will always try and put as many bodies in front of him as possible to obstruct his view of the puck. Trying to find a little black disc through a mess of sticks, legs and skates makes the goaltender's job all the more difficult, and even if the goalie does spot the puck through the traffic, it is more likely to be deflected.

Trailer: A player who follows the action of the play seemingly from a safe distance but is actually at the ready for a drop or blind pass.

T

Trap: While firewagon hockey best describes a style of hockey centered purely on scoring as many goals as possible, the trap is a style of hockey that is focused on keeping the puck out of a team's zone and out of the net. With the trap, defense is the key. While good defense has been part of the game since it began, the trap was a system that was not widely used until the mid-1990s.

Players hate it and fans are bored by it, but using the trap has proven to be an effective way to win hockey games. In the late 1990s, with the proliferation of new franchises in the National Hockey League, it became very competitive for general managers to sign talented players, leaving some teams such as the Detroit Red Wings with an all-star lineup, while new teams such as the Florida Panthers languished in the basement of the league. To compensate for the discrepancy, coaches with the "less-talented" teams had to work around the system, and soon the neutral zone trap was born.

The trap is easily explained. Take two teams, for example, the Detroit Red Wings versus the New Jersey Devils. When the Devils take an early lead on a goal by Claude Lemieux, that's when head coach Jacques Lemaire puts the neutral zone

T

trap into effect. Sergei Fedorov and Steve Yzer-
man break out of their zone on the rush but are
stopped by a formidable wall in the neutral
zone led by master defensemen Scott Stevens
and Scott Niedermayer. Every time Detroit tries
to break into the Devils' zone, the puck carrier
faces a wall of players blocking his way. The odd
time the Red Wings do get into the zone to set
up for a shot, they are met by the stellar goaltending of Martin Brodeur. The Devils end up
winning with a score of 2–1 and most of their
other games by similar close margins. When the
Devils defeated the Detroit Red Wings in the
1995 playoffs to win the Stanley Cup for the first
time in history, weaker teams saw that the trap
provided less offensive-minded teams a way to
stay competitive.

Another team that based its play around the trap,
the Florida Panthers used the style to get all the
way to the Stanley Cup finals in 1996, only to lose
in four straight games to the Colorado Avalanche.

Veteran defenseman Gary Suter started his
career during the high-scoring days of the 1980s
and ended it during the height of the days of the
trap and was never shy in hiding his disdain for it.
"You started to see it more and more as expan-
sion grew," said the San Jose Sharks defenseman.

"With the talent level being watered down, teams had to figure out a way to shut down the opposition. When a team is successful at something, it becomes a trend, and that's exactly what happened. It started with New Jersey and then moved around the rest of the league. Now everyone does it." (*Hockey Digest*, January 1, 2001, Chris Anderson)

Always good for an interview, Jeremy Roenick once said of the trap in a post-game interview after a particularly defensive match in which he was held scoreless: "Whoever invented the trap should be shot!"

While the league has tried to make changes to the rules of the game and have referees apply them to the letter, defensive systems will always be a part of the sport, and no matter what the league does to increase scoring, coaches will always work around it if they need to.

Firewagon hockey versus the trap

1985–1986 (before the trap became popular): Thirteen players finished the season with more than 100 points, with Wayne Gretzky leading the way with 215 (a league record). Five players scored 50 goals or more, with the Oilers Jarri Kurri at the top with 68 goals. Goaltender Bob

T

Froese of the Philadelphia Flyers led the league with the lowest goals-against average of 2.55, followed by Al Jensen of the Washington Capitals at 3.18.

1998–1999 (the height of the trap's popularity): Only three players finished the regular season with over 100 points. Jaromir Jagr topped the list with 127 points. Paul Kariya got the most goals that season with 47. Goaltender Ron Tugnutt won the lowest goals-against average race, finishing the regular season at 1.79, while Dominik Hasek of the Buffalo Sabres was not far behind with a 1.87 goals-against average.

Trapper: A goaltender's glove, worn on the free hand. Emile "the Cat" Francis can be credited with the invention of the goalie glove, or trapper. Tired of having the puck slip through his fingers, Francis decided to test league regulations during a game against the Detroit Red Wings by wearing a modified first baseman's mitt in net. Detroit coach Jack Adams protested the new contraption, saying that it did not belong in hockey, but league president Clarence Campbell approved the new equipment. Soon goaltenders across the league were frustrating goal scorers and entertaining fans with their flashy glove saves. The modern-day glove is much bigger than the one first used by Francis and is much better designed to protect the goaltender's wrist and hand.

Tripping: An infraction in which a player uses a part of his body to knock the feet out from under another player. It carries a sentence of two-minutes in the sin bin.

Turnover: When the team in possession of the puck gives the puck to their opponents. This usually occurs when one player makes a mistake such as a bad pass or loses the puck on a check or a soft dump-in.

Turtle: In the wild, when a turtle is threatened or attacked by a larger, more aggressive predator, it will quickly retreat into its own shell for protection, thus saving itself from harm. In hockey, a turtle is a player, who when challenged to a fight by an opponent, immediately falls to the ice in the fetal position and covers his head to protect it from the punches of the aggressor. Turtle-ing is rather uncommon in the National Hockey League because it is considered a cowardly act.

While there have been many turtles in the NHL, none are more famous than Claude Lemieux. During his long career, Lemieux put his hands to

T

his head and tucked his knees close to his chin on many occasions, but none more famous than his mix-up with Darren McCarty of the Detroit Red Wings. The story starts during the 1996 Conference finals between Lemieux's Colorado Avalanche and the Red Wings on May 29. Lemieux became Detroit public enemy number one when he checked the Wings Kris Draper from behind, sending him face-first into the boards. Draper suffered a broken jaw and a bloody face in the incident, while Lemieux only received a two-game suspension. The Avalanche went on to win the Stanley Cup, but the Red Wings never forgot what Lemieux did to their teammate.

On March 26, 1997, after waiting for just the right moment, Red Wing Darren McCarty sought out his retribution for the vicious hit on his teammate in the first period of the game in front of the partisan crowd at Detroit's Joe Louis Arena. But McCarty would be denied a satisfying revenge, because at the moment he dropped his glove to attack, Lemieux fell to his knees and assumed the turtle position. The opinion is widely held that, according to the unwritten code of conduct in the NHL, Lemieux should have stood up and fought McCarty for what he did to Draper.

Twig: Another term for a hockey stick. See "branch."

Twine minder: A goaltender.

Two-line pass: With the new rule that removed the center red line from play, the two-line pass is no longer part of the game. Before the rule was introduced in the 2005–06 season, a two-line pass was when a player in his team's defensive zone passed the puck over his own blue line to a teammate who had already crossed the center red line. The play was whistled down by the referee and a faceoff was taken in the offending team's zone.

Two-on-one: An offensive rush. Two players from one team break quickly down the ice to attack the opposing team's net with just one opposing player back to defend.

Two-platoon goalkeeping: Before the 1960s, most teams used to dress just one goaltender in their starting lineup. But as the league expanded and the number of games increased, the demands on the lone goaltender in the lineup

T

proved to be too much, so teams started dressing two goaltenders for each game. The two-goaltender system became known as two-platoon goalkeeping, though the term is never used today.

T

Undressed: Can refer to a player or a goaltender. When a player or goaltender is completely fooled by another player's sweet stick-handling moves, he has been undressed. As the word naturally suggests to the imagination, it can be very embarrassing when a player is undressed in front of thousands of screaming fans.

U

Waffle pad: Also known as the goaltender's blocker. It is the large, rectangular pad attached to the goaltender's stick hand.

Wash out: A referee's arm motion when a goal is ruled invalid or to wave off an infraction. The ref will usually swing his arms outward in a "washing out" motion to signal to the players that the play was ruled invalid.

Wheels: Refers to a player's skating ability. An excellent skater is said to have great wheels.

Wicket: Another term borrowed from cricket. In cricket, it describes the three posts and two bails that are positioned behind the batter. When hockey first began, it was a hybrid of many sports and did not really have its own name. In the absence of any concrete name for the new game, the word wicket was used to describe what would be come to known as hockey.

Wings: The left and right wings are the two players that flank the center on the forward attacking line.

Wrap around: One of the most annoying goals for a goaltender to let in. A wrap around occurs when a player takes the puck behind the net and tries to come around quickly from the side to slide the puck into the goal. The move can be very effective because it forces the goaltender to quickly move laterally from one side to another, and if the player can confuse the goaltender as to which side he will attempt to put the puck in, then he will have a better chance of scoring on the wrap around.

Wrist shot/Wrister: A type of shot in which the player uses a strong flick of the wrist and the forearm to shoot the puck. A wrist shot is much slower but far more accurate than a slapshot.

W

X-ray vision: A goaltender that is able to see the puck through the traffic in front of his net and make the save is said to have x-ray vision.

Yawning cage: This colorful term simply describes a wide-open net. This can occur when a goaltender is caught out of position or when the net is empty. "Jagr shot the puck into the yawning cage."

Z

Zamboni: The wonderful machine fans see at hockey games between periods that magically scrapes off a layer of ice and replaces it with a shiny, wet, new surface. The Zamboni was invented by Frank Zamboni and has become an integral part of hockey culture since it first appeared in 1949. There are other companies that produce ice resurfacers, but it is the Zamboni machine that has worked its way into hearts and minds of hockey fans everywhere.

Zambonis: An American musical quartet founded by Dave Schneider and billed as "the greatest, and only, hockey rock band."

Zebra: Because of their black-and-white-striped uniforms, the referee is often referred to as a zebra.

Zone: A team's end of the ice.

Z

Hockey Rink

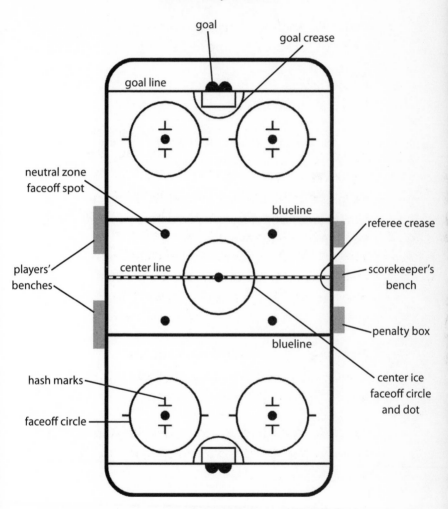

Resource List

Podnieks, Andrew. *The Life and Times of Wayne Gretzky*. Chicago: Triumph Books, 1999.

Roche, Bill, ed. *The Hockey Book*. Toronto: McClelland and Stewart, 1953.

Spencer, David and Barbara. *The Pocket Hockey Encyclopedia*. Toronto: Pagurian Press, 1976.

Vaughan, Garth. *The Puck Starts Her*e. Fredericton, New Brunswick: Goose Lane Editions and Four East Publications, 1996.

Authors

David John

David John is a writer, photographer and enthu-siastic follower of hockey. He developed a passion for the sport after seeing his first Montreal Cana-diens game. His best memory is of getting to go into the 1979 Montreal Canadiens dressing room after a game and seeing all the greats such as Guy Lafleur, Steve Shutt and Ken Dryden (whose arms were covered in bruises from all the pucks).

He has a BA in political science from McGill University, and a graduate diploma in journalism from Concordia University. He currently lives just outside the city of Montreal.

Brian Kennedy

Born in Montreal, Brian spent much of his hockey-playing youth in Ontario. He went school in the U.S. in 1981 and ended up in Los Angeles. He's been a hockey fan since the age of five and played hockey as a child, retiring three different times.

Brian holds a PhD in English and teaches at Pasadena City College. He is also a freelance sportswriter, using his writing to get him everywhere from NHL locker rooms to the race shops of famous drivers of the past and present. He covers the Anaheim Ducks and the LA Kings, and in his spare time he rides a racing bike, practices karate and preserves memories.